WORDS ON MUSIC

By the same author

Time for Lovers

Robin Ray's Music Quiz

Favourite Hymns and Carols

Words on Music

Collected by

ROBIN RAY

Methuen

First published in Great Britain 1984
by Methuen London Ltd.
11 New Fetter Lane, London EC4P 4EE
Individual contributions © as indicated in Acknowledgements
This compilation © 1984 by Robin Ray

Set in 11 point IBM Journal by 🅰 Tek-Art, Croydon, Surrey
Printed in Great Britain by
Richard Clay (The Chaucer Press) Ltd,
Bungay, Suffolk

British Library Cataloguing in Publication Data

Words on music.
  1. Musicians — Biography
  I. Ray, Robin
  780'.903   ML385

ISBN 0-413-53940-7

FOR MAMMA

Prelude

I have always loved music, mainly, I suppose, because it was always there for me to love. When I was a child music was used rather like a patent medicine. Mummy would sing you to sleep at night and rock you and croon to you when you were unwell. Today it is a quick spoonful of crushed-up junior aspirin. Not that I have a rooted objection to taking medicine when the body needs it; it is just that many complaints require a prescription of a more personal nature, and music can, perhaps even should, be part of that. Music is the medicine of the soul.

Family legend has it that when I was born the matron of the nursing home told my parents I was 'the worst baby this place has ever seen'; perhaps I had taken the notion that I was one of the 'poor banished children of Eve; in this vale of tears' literally, because I bawled without respite from morning to night. Endless cures were tried, but one, and only one, proved effective — my father had to play his violin. For six months the unfortunate man gave a series of recitals, rare if not unique in musical history. Unaccompanied, and unpaid, he played his heart out, in concerts given at all hours and at a moment's notice, the repertoire encompassing all he knew from memory, from Kreisler's 'Schon Rosmarin' through 'Sweet and Low' to 'Where the Blue of the Night Meets the Gold of the Day', which I'm sorry to say it often did.

When my father was away on tour, telling jokes and playing his violin to grown-up audiences (whose sleep he dreaded), my mother would sing to me instead. In bed:

'Just a song at twilight, when the lights are low,
And the flickering shadows softly come and go.'

In the kitchen:

'Knees up Mother Brown, knees up Mother Brown;
Under the table you must go.'

In the bath:

'Alice was very slender, Alice was very slim,
She went into the bathroom, put the plug in and jumped
    right in.
Her maid, who was absent-minded, pulled the plug out
    before she was through,
Oh! Pussyfoot-Johnson, save my soul, there goes Alice
    down the hole,
Alice! . . . Where are you going?'

When we went with Dad on tour, they sang in the car:

'With someone like you, a pal good and true,
I'd like to leave it all behind,
And go and find
A place that's known to God alone,
Just a spot to call our own.'

When I wasn't taken on tour I stayed with my grandmother.
She played the piano and was happy to play and sing to me
every night if I asked her — Victorian songs of alternating
agony and ecstasy, which always ended beyond the tomb.
Add to all this the wind-up gramophone ('My Old Flame'),
the cinema (I saw my first screen musical, *Roman Scandals*,
when I was 18 months of age), and Sunday School ('You in
Your Small Corner, and I in Mine') — I must have known at
least a hundred songs before I was 5.

It was then I saw Eric Ogden.

Eric Ogden was the conductor of the pit orchestra in one

of the theatres where my father was appearing on stage, and from the moment I first saw him, immaculate in tail suit, complete with red carnation and white baton, I had eyes for no one else. The massed forces under his command couldn't have been far in excess of fourteen players, but I had never heard so many musicians 'live' before and the sound and sight of them thrilled me beyond description.

'Could I come to band call?' I asked my father. 'And see the rehearsals? And sit near Eric Ogden? And can I have a conductor's stick?' Dad granted the first two wishes, but not the third and, as I sat in the front row of the stalls with my baton substitute, Eric Ogden looked at me over his shoulder and said, 'Four in a bar, you. All right?' as if we were partners. I was in heaven.

It would be satisfying if I could say that, from that moment on I made up my mind to become a conductor, or at least earn my living in the theatre or through music, but it wouldn't be true. The birth of my ambition to be a conductor you can, if you care to, read of later in this collection, but the point I wish to make here has not so much to do with music as with heroes, because heroes are, to a large extent, what this book is about.

I suppose you could quibble that the title *Words on Music* is misleading because I have both extended and exceeded my self-imposed brief. The original intention was to compile a collection solely of literary descriptions of music, showing how through the ages men and women have sought, with varying degress of success, to describe something which is by nature indescribable. Such a project is perfectly feasible but I soon tired of the restrictive and unreasonable disciplines which the task imposed.

Music does not exist by itself. It is the product of people and it follows that the process which creates it cannot be divorced from life. This was brought home to me with some force when I was rereading for inclusion in the book the letter from Tchaikovsky to his friend and patroness Nadejda von Meck in which he attempts to explain the 'programme' of

3

his Fourth Symphony. He speaks of Fate, constantly and unswervingly poisoning the soul; of grief and irreparable loss; of being alone and sad when in a crowd. Surely, I thought, no one can seek to express such feelings in music unless they are part of their previous experience. It was then that I was reminded of the year the symphony was written, 1877, the year of the composer's hastily arranged and disastrous marriage which he underwent in a desperate attempt to cure his homosexuality, and which finally drove him to attempt suicide. So alongside this letter you will find letters about his wife; both tell you the story of the symphony.

Of course, I am well aware that relating life to music is not always necessary and that, indeed, it can be carried too far. Although it may be illuminating to know that Beethoven went deaf and Schumann went mad, it is not essential to one's appreciation of Puccini's *La Bohème* to know that the composer enjoyed slaughtering large numbers of wildfowl.

Passion — ultimately and inevitably — became the dominant factor in compiling this collection, which is a small sample not so much of what I have read over the years as what I have remembered reading, and this brings me back full circle to heroes. You will find many (though by no means all) of my heroes in the pages which follow. Some, like Chopin and Dinu Lipatti, are given a disproportionate amount of space, though I have no more consciously striven to exclude those who do not profoundly affect me (Vivaldi, Janáček and Alkan) than to include those (Mozart, Ravel and Rachmaninoff) who do. I have allowed myself the same eccentric freedom with regard to subject matter and it will doubtless be noted that peculiar fascinations exist in this area too — pianists, love, film music, conductors, death — and the inability to pass up a good story.

Where the extracts have required some explanation or linking I have added the odd remark, which I hope will prove helpful, but in the main I have attempted to arrange the material in such a way that one piece naturally follows on from, or leads to, another.

4

Reading it through, though, it is hard to avoid the conclusion that, in the final analysis, it is a book about myself.

Robin Ray
Brighton, 1984

We are the music-makers,
    And we are the dreamers of dreams,
Wandering by lone sea-breakers,
    And sitting by desolate streams;
World-losers and world-forsakers,
    On whom the pale moon gleams:
But we are the movers and shakers
    Of the world for ever, it seems.

Arthur William Edgar O'Shaughnessy

You know, the critics never change; I'm still getting the same notices I used to get as a child. They tell me I play very well for my age. . . .

Mischa Elman

For a year or so they* lived as cheaply as was possible in a rooming house, and found the only diversion they could safely afford in themselves. Bronx Park in fact did duty as their Eden and they would walk through it singing Hebrew songs as though they were Adam and Eve and their language the names of every beast and fowl. My coming announced their fall from self-sufficiency. Obliged to find an apartment of their own, they searched the neighbourhood and after several disappointments chose one within walking distance of the park. Showing them out after they had viewed it, the landlady observed, with every intention of pleasing her new tenants and clinching the bargain, 'And you'll be glad to know I don't take Jews.' History, in New York at any rate, has muffled that voice, but how bitterly in my parents' ears must have sounded the hostility which, having propelled them to the shores of the New World, had followed them there! Her mistake made clear to her, the anti-Semitic landlady was renounced and another apartment found, where in due course they gathered friends about them, fellow students

*Menuhin's parents.

7

and other young people as poor and light-hearted as themselves, who created a cheerful haven against prejudice. But the landlady's blunder left its mark. Back on the street, my mother took a vow: her unborn child would wear a label proclaiming his race to the world. He would be called 'the Jew'.

Yehudi Menuhin
Unfinished Journey

There can be no doubt that Kreisler's strong personality has contributed to his enormous popularity: his bearing on the platform and that kindly smile have done much to win the favour of his audiences. His generosity, too, will long be remembered. After the Great War, for instance, he gave the greater part of his income to the alleviation of distress in his native Austria, and his wife undertook personal responsibility for over forty war orphans. For five years he contributed handsomely towards the support of 1,500 starving artists.

Many other musicians have reason to be grateful to him for kindly acts and assistance in times of need. An example of the sort of thing he used to do will be found in an incident that took place during one of his visits to Dublin. Walking along one of the main streets in very bad weather he was vexed to hear a talented young lady playing the violin in the gutter. He stood for a few minutes listening as she played in the rain, and then told her that he would find her a job. Of course, he had no idea how to start this undertaking, but he did not rest until he had secured for her a permanent post in a theatre orchestra.

He has always been unmoved by the favours and patronage of royalty, and showed little enthusiasm for their invitations unless they happened to be genuinely interested in music. On the other hand, he has invariably been keen to meet great scientists, philosophers, painters and writers when on his

8

travels, whether they have been interested in music or not. His interest in science, medicine and surgery is well known, but few of his admirers realise that he can speak no fewer than eight modern languages, and has also a good knowledge of Latin and Greek. Incidentally, he is a fervent collector of rare books.

His spontaneous wit makes him an ever-welcome guest at the houses of his many friends, and he delights in good company, but he loathes invitations to play at private parties held by prominent members of society. In his earlier days, particularly when he was in his prime as a virtuoso, he received dozens of such invitations and tried to discourage people from sending them by charging very high fees. On one occasion a fabulously wealthy lady demanded his services, and would not be deterred even when he quoted a fee of $3,000 for playing just a few little pieces. So he accepted the engagement. The lady then told him that she did not wish him to mix with her guests, many of whom would be very prominent people, and he replied immediately: 'In that case, madam, my fee will be only $2,000.'

Donald Brook
Violinists of Today

Dear Mr Ray,

First of all I wish to thank you for your programme on Jascha Heifetz.* Recently I retired from the viola section of the RPO (of which I was a founder member).

During my long life as an orchestral player (with the LPO in 1934!) I have had many experiences of playing with Heifetz and have even spoken to him on several occasions — rather like speaking to God! How many times have I got myself thoroughly incensed when people have called his

*A profile of the violinist on BBC Radio 4, 1980.

playing cold — this happened a lot in the early years. I even possessed the recording of the Bazzini (how I wish I had it now).

The last time I recorded with him was I think in 1965 with the *ad hoc* orchestra at Walthamstow when every violinist who could manage it came and sat around the walls. On that occasion he recorded the Bloch Scottish Fantasia and a Vieuxtemps concerto. My feelings during that week of sessions were, as with all the seasonal players, that the man was transcendental — in fact seemed to be from another sphere, and I am not prone to that kind of experience. People were walking about in a kind of daze at the end of the last session.

At one point in the slow movement in the Bloch he did his famous Heifetz portamento (which everybody unsuccessfully tried to emulate) to a top note which was so lovely that many people let out a sigh and Heifetz said in his American accent, 'Well, fellows — we'll have to do that again.'

That is one story to add to your collection.

Another time in 1950 at the Carnegie Hall (during the famous tour of the USA with Beecham, Nathan Milstein and Isaac Stern happened to be in the green-room during a rehearsal break when some wag put on a recording of Heifetz playing the Scherzo — Tarantella by Wieniawski and, I am not sure whether it was Milstein or Stern who said: 'Turn that bastard off!' and we all collapsed with laughter.

John Myers
18 February, 1980

Jacques Thibaud was one of our important visitors in the symphony concert season of 1903 when he came over to play the Third Saint-Saëns Violin Concerto. A delightful, fascinating man. No matter in what part of the world one comes across him he seems to be surrounded by an enormous

10

circle of friends. I think it was entirely owing to him that the French conferred on me the coveted *Officier du Légion d'Honneur* in 1926.

Some years later, I had been conducting concerts in Monte Carlo and found Cortot was giving a recital with Thibaud. Cortot invited us (with Thibaud) to lunch. There was a large bottle of champagne on the sideboard but during the meal we only drank red wine. Thibaud kept eyeing this champagne. At last he could endure it no longer. . . .

'What about that champagne, Cortot?' he asked. 'You have forgotten it.'

Cortot murmured: 'So I have!'

'I am good at opening champagne bottles,' announced Thibaud. He then proceeded to prove the assertion. When I saw him later in the evening he dug me in the ribs. 'I wasn't going to have that champagne standing there and then put back in the cellar!'

I met those two again in Edinburgh at the house of Methven Simpson after one of his concerts. Simpson was a true friend to art in Edinburgh. He had a music shop in Princes Street. His wife was French and, like most of her compatriots, was skilled in the art of cooking — a fact which both Thibaud and Cortot appreciated. For that matter, I did myself, and enjoyed many a delightful dinner with them. Thibaud was playing at a symphony concert at Queen's Hall soon after his happy meeting in Edinburgh. During the interval a quietly-spoken distinguished-looking man asked permission to see M. Thibaud.

'No you can't,' snapped Newman* — who was guarding the artist's room door — 'come after the concert if you like.'

The visitor returned after the concert to be greeted by Thibaud: 'Ah, your Majesty, you did then come to hear me play,' and then introduced us to the King of Portugal.

Henry J. Wood
My Life of Music

*Robert Newman (Concert promoter, and creator of the promenade concerts.)

In 1907 Wood invited Max Reger to lunch during that composer's visit to this country. Knowing his partiality for beer at mealtimes, Wood ordered two dozen bottles. He recalled in *My Life of Music* that Reger consumed *most* of the beer provided, and then had four glasses of whisky and soda after the meal. That afternoon he drove down to the German Club with the intention, Sir Henry said, of getting a drink.

Donald Brook
The Life of Sir Henry Wood

I met Toscanini once or twice and he never talked about music at all. I remember a story told to me by Bill Primrose, who used to play Willie Walton's Viola Concerto and was principal viola player under Toscanini in New York. One day after rehearsal the maestro said: 'Primrose, you will come to dinner with me tonight. My wife is away and so we shall be alone.' Primrose nearly fainted. To think that he was going to have an evening with the maestro! He would hear all about how Toscanini began his career, how he played, as a second-desk cellist, in the first performance of Verdi's *Otello*. He was going to have a wonderful evening.

He goes to Toscanini's house. They're alone, with the butler in attendance. Toscanini gobbles up his spaghetti, swallows his chianti without a word, and then rushes into the television room. He turns to the station that features wrestling and watches with a non-stop verbal accompaniment: 'Hit 'im in ze stomm-ahk. Get 'im by ze leg. Jomp on 'im.' Poor Primrose. Music was never discussed.

Neville Cardus
Conversations with Cardus

After the last evening at the Châtelet, Emmy Destinn invited me for supper in her suite at the Hotel Regina, where she stayed with her sister. They changed into their dressing-gowns, and the three of us sat down to a snack of cold meat and champagne. I expressed my admiration of her art to the great singer and cited some particularly impressive moments in her *Aïda, Carmen,* and, now *Salomé.*

'The way you sing is a great lesson for me,' I said. 'You taught me how to use judiciously the rubato, that much misunderstood definition of the free expression of a melody. I try to translate your perfect breathing control into my own phrasing, and I feel certain that Chopin had exactly that on his mind when he required rubato in his works.'

Emmy Destinn listened to my long talk with frowning attention, but suddenly she picked up her glass of champagne and smashed it to bits against the fireplace.

'All right, all right,' she screamed, in a rage. 'I know I am a good singer, but I am also a woman!'

I was aghast. Her sister stood up calmly and left the room, and here I was, with Pola in my heart and on my mind, expected to prove that I was a man, too! She was a strange woman, Emmy Destinn. And she really frightened me when I saw the threatening head of a serpent on her thigh. She had a bright-coloured tattoo of a boa encircling her leg from the ankle to the upper thigh; it took me some time to get over my shock. I am afraid I was not at my best that night, but she seemed not to mind; later she became quite mellow and maternal.

Artur Rubinstein
My Young Years

The sound of a harpsichord: two skeletons copulating on a galvanised tin roof.

Sir Thomas Beecham

I never practise; I always play.

Wanda Landowska
Time, 1 December 1952

If I don't practise for one day, I know it;
if I don't practise for two days, the critics know it;
if I don't practise for three days, the audience knows it.

Ignace Jan Paderewski

Paderewski in Manchester

It was a moving experience to listen to Paderewski on Saturday evening, and we think the famous musician himself must have been deeply stirred by the feelings of affection as well as admiration expressed by the great crowd in the Free Trade Hall. What memories his presence evokes, and what an atmosphere of romance surrounds him — the man who, after breaking off a long and gorgeous musical career in order to become a political leader in wartime, resumed his pianoforte playing and in spite of advancing age established himself again as the prince of pianists! Do the young folk among the crowd who heard him on Saturday wonder why some of us still think of him as the player and the personality who more certainly than any of the later brilliant exponents of the instrument followed in Liszt's steps? They would understand if they could have a true idea of Paderewski when he brought to his recitals a sense not only of the most vivid and trenchant artistry but of something which in its own nature was more intrepid than any quality in the art of his rivals. He was, indeed, a supremely heroic figure in the musical world, just as Liszt had been, and, as often happens when great personalities are concerned, legend combined with actual historical fact in spreading the fame of Paderewski's achievements.

The strain, however, of long-continued periods of work, anxiety, and responsibility is bound in the end to take its toll, and we see that during the last few years Paderewski has become an old man. Till now we have never thought of him as growing old. He is rich in honours and he is the possessor of a garnered knowledge of music which shows itself in many a quiet yet telling reach of expression and especially in the confidence with which he follows certain kinds of reflective music into its recesses of thought and emotion; but the pianist's fingers do not now convey all that his mind and heart have conceived. In Bach's Chromatic Fantasia and Fugue he kept within a small range of tone and dwelt lovingly on what is meditative and withdrawn from outward show in the content of each movement. The playing was wholly intro-spective. At times the pianist seemed to be musing on Bach's themes without thought of whether an audience were heeding or not, and not always were phrases or the notes forming them delivered clearly. How characteristic was his dallying over the cadences! During the last few years he has suggested more wistfully than ever the idea of retrospect in his cadential chords.

From Bach the pianist went to Haydn and Mozart, the former master heard in the F minor Variations, the latter in his Rondo in A minor. The performance was uneven, yet it showed both verve and delicacy. There was grace in the phrasing. The so-called 'Moonlight' Sonata of Beethoven was given without the emphasis on melodic singing tone usually heard in the opening movement and without the technical security in later parts which only a little time ago was as definitely a feature of the player's style as it is in the equipment of famous younger artists. Arresting passages were frequent. Again Paderewski seemed to be almost oblivious of his audience. He was preoccupied with the spirit of the work and not with its outward forms. Schubert's Impromptu in A flat, with the flowing middle section in D flat, was made to disclose much of its poetry, and a nocturne, a waltz, and a mazurka by Chopin were given with something of the player's former glamour of style. The power and velocity required in Chopin's A flat Polonaise and in Liszt's Second Rhapsody could not be expected. As an encore number Liszt's arrangement of Isolde's closing scene from *Tristan* was given. The recital had pathetic elements. It was haunted by ghosts and echoes of the past.

G.A.H.
Newspaper review
Manchester

In my attempts to trace the date of that article (circa 1937) I turned to a quaint but useful book, A Musical Gazetteer of Great Britain and Northern Ireland, *which, under regional headings, gives information of which towns musicians have been born in, died in or visited.*

Franz Liszt, *mentioned in the Paderewski review and by general consent assumed to be the greatest pianist of all time, also features in the* Gazetteer, *indeed he tops all the other entries in the index, even though his listings are by no means comprehensive. He was an indefatigable traveller, but a combination of some of the dates of one of his tours in the 1840s exposes a less glamorous trip than we might have imagined — funny, sad and tedious by turns, with the last entry a little of all three.*

16

Franz Liszt, having been sick while crossing the Solent, played at a concert in Ryde Town Hall on 18 August 1840, stayed briefly at the Star Hotel and, later in the day, played on a cottage piano in another concert, at the Green Dragon Hotel, Newport, where he stayed the night. He embarked the next day from Cowes for Southampton.

Exmouth   Franz Liszt played at a concert here on 24 August 1840.

Torquay   Franz Liszt stayed here on 25 August 1840. He had intended to take part in a concert, but this had to be cancelled because he was too unwell to perform.

Plymouth   Franz Liszt played at a concert here on 26 August 1840. He remained in the city for the next day and night and left for Exeter at 8 a.m. on the 28th. A projected concert on the 27th was cancelled when only seven people bought tickets.

Boston   Franz Liszt played at a concert in The Peacock and Royal Hotel on 14 September 1840. He stayed the night there. The site of the hotel, in Market Place, is now occupied by Boots.

Newmarket   Franz Liszt, travelling from Cambridge to Bury St Edmunds, had breakfast here on 19 September 1840.

Halford   Franz Liszt, travelling from Oxford to Royal Leamington Spa, had luncheon here on 25 November 1840.

Birmingham   Franz Liszt played at a concert in the Old Royal Hotel (demolished) on 26 November 1840 and, according to one of his travelling companions, John Orlando Parry, 'broke three strings on one note'. He had dinner at Dea's Royal Hotel and afterwards felt unwell.

Nantwich   Franz Liszt, travelling from Newcastle-under-Lyme to Chester, had luncheon at The Crown on 29 November 1840.

Chester   Franz Liszt stayed at the Royal Hotel on the nights of 29 and 30 November 1840. He took part in a concert there on the 30th. When walking to see the cathedral, he excited astonishment among the citizens of Chester by wearing an enormous Hungarian coat made of many different skins and brightly coloured leathers, with matching cap.

Hebden Bridge Franz Liszt, travelling from York to Manchester, had luncheon, consisting of ham and eggs, at The White Lion on 15 December 1840.

Liverpool Franz Liszt played at a concert in the Theatre Royal on 1 December 1840. He stayed the night at The Feathers, Clayton Square. On 16 December 1840 he had luncheon at The Queen's Arms before embarking for Dublin.

Dublin Franz Liszt stayed at Morrison's Leinster Hotel, in Dawson Street, 17-26 December 1840, playing in three concerts at the Rotunda. On the 17th he saw Charles Kean, the son of Edmund Kean, in *Macbeth*. On 18 December he performed Weber's Konzertstück and his own transcription of the overture to *William Tell;* on 21 December a *Lucia di Lammermoor* transcription and the 'Grand Galop chromatique'; on 23 December the *Hexaméron* and extemporisations on John Orlando Parry's 'Wanted, a Governess', an Irish folk-song and the Russian national anthem, combining all three melodies in an astonishing finale. On the 24th he had dinner with Lord Morpeth.

Clonmel Franz Liszt, travelling from Kilkenny to Cork, had luncheon in the Commercial Room on 27 December 1840. He returned on 2 January 1841, intending to take part in a concert in the Court House, but not a single ticket had been sold. He therefore invited a few music lovers to his hotel, where he and the other members of his concert party went through their entire programme. He used the modest hotel piano: 'So funny to see Liszt firing away at *Guillaume Tell* on this little instrument,' wrote John Orlando Parry, 'but it stood his powerful hand capitally.'

While in the town of Laurence Sterne's birth, the composer

may have visited the home of his friend Lady Blessington,* one of the most beautiful women of her day. A secluded stretch of the River Suir at Clonmel is known as 'Lady Blessington's Bath', where she used to bathe.

Fermoy Franz Liszt, travelling from Kilkenny to Cork, had supper at The Queen's Arms on 27 December 1840. Returning to Kilkenny, he had supper again here on 1 January 1841.

Cork Franz Liszt stayed at the Imperial Clarence Hotel 28 December 1940—1 January 1841. At a concert in the hotel on 28 December he played a *Lucia di Lammermoor* transcription, his transcription of the overture to *William Tell* and the 'Grand Galop chromatique'. On 29 December he visited Cobh, where he had a lunch of oysters and turkey at the Navy Hotel. At a concert in the Imperial Clarence on 30 December he extemporised on Lover's 'Rory O'More' and Moore's 'The Last Rose of Summer' and played a *Norma* transcription. On 31 December he visited the cemetery and lunatic asylum in company with other musicians. On 1 January, he played in a third concert here.

Carlow Franz Liszt, travelling from Kilkenny to Dublin, had luncheon here on 3 January 1841.

Naas Franz Liszt, travelling from Kilkenny to Dublin, had tea here on the afternoon of 3 January 1841.

Roscrea Franz Liszt, travelling from Dublin to Limerick, had supper here on 8 January 1841. Returning from Limerick, he had breakfast here on 12 January.

Limerick Franz List stayed at the Royal Mail Hotel 9—12 January 1841. On the 9th he played at a concert in Swinburne's Great Rooms and had dinner at the home of the Police General, Mr Vaux, with whom he again dined on the 10th. On the 11th he took part in a second concert in Swinburne's Great Rooms.

---

* 'What a pity to put such a handsome man to a piano!' she once said of him.

Monasterevin Franz Liszt, travelling from Dublin to Limerick, had luncheon at Fleming's Hotel on 8 January 1841. Returning from Limerick on 12 January, he again had luncheon here.

Drogheda Franz Liszt, travelling from Dublin to Belfast, had afternoon tea here on 14 January 1841.

Newry Franz Liszt, travelling from Dublin to Belfast, spent the night of 14 January 1841 here.

Donaghadee Franz Liszt spent his last night in Ireland, 16 January 1841, here before embarking for Scotland.

Stranraer Franz Liszt spent the night of 17 January 1841 here, having earlier in the day disembarked from Ireland at Portpatrick. At 5 a.m. on the following morning he boarded the *Sir William Wallace* steam packet and sailed for Ayr.

Ayr Franz Liszt disembarked here at about 10a.m. on the morning of 18 January 1841, having sailed from Stranraer in the *Sir William Wallace* steam packet. A great deal of snow had recently fallen, and it was bitterly cold. After taking some nourishment at The King's Arms, he left a 11a.m. in an open third-class train, carrying cattle and pigs, and arrived in Glasgow at 2 p.m.

Glasgow Franz Liszt, travelling from Ayr to Edinburgh, stayed at the George Hotel, George Square, during the afternoon and evening of 18 January 1841. He returned on 20 January and played at a concert. He stayed the night here and left for Edinburgh in the morning. He took part in a second concert, on the 22nd, arriving, according to John Orlando Parry, with 'some very dashing Scottish girls'.

Edinburgh Franz Liszt played at a concert in the Assembly Rooms in George Street on 19 January 1841. He stayed the night at The Royal Hotel (demolished) in Princes Street. After visiting Glasgow on the 20th, he played at a second concert on the 21st, every piece being encored. He had dinner, that evening, at the home of the music publisher Robert

20

Paterson. After a second visit to Glasgow, he took part in a third concert at the Hopetoun Rooms, now the hall of the Mary Erskine School, in Queen Street on the 23rd. He left Edinburgh on 24 January.

Dunbar Franz Liszt, travelling from Edinburgh, stopped here for dinner and went to see Dunbar Castle on the evening of 24 January 1841.

Berwick-upon-Tweed Franz Liszt had supper here on the evening of 24 January 1841.

Darlington Franz Liszt took part in a concert here on 27 January 1841 (during the course of which an inebriate offered him a sovereign to play 'Rule, Britannia').

Gerald Norris

Career of a Virtuoso

Where is my Bradshaw? How do I get there?
　　Ah! Page a hundred: here's the only train.
Change — can I risk it? Three minutes to spare.
　　No sleeping car? Well, useless to complain.

Next morning at eleven, half awake
　　And shivering, I arrive. A man comes up.
'Make haste! Rehearsal's waiting! You must take
　　A cab at once!' No time for bite or sup.

No time to change or wash. 'You're rather late,'
　　Says the presiding magnate. 'You must know
The rehearsal's public. We have had to wait;
　　The songs were all sung half an hour ago.'

Straight to the platform — play as best I can —
  Hungry and dirty, fingers frozen quite —
That's done! Why, there's the critic! 'Poor old man,
  You can't expect him to go out at night.'

The concert's a success — but what of that?
  The critic writes on how *he* heard me play.
Encore? No time. I seize my coat and hat,
  For to the station it's a goodish way.

Into the train just as the whistle blows —
  On to the next place, supperless again,
Clammy with sweating, still in evening clothes —
  Tomorrow the rehearsal is at ten.

Ferruccio Busoni
Translated by E.J. Dent

The notes I handle no better than many pianists. But the pauses between the notes — ah, that is where the art resides!

Artur Schnabel
Chicago *Daily News*, 11 June 1958

Claudio Arrau *expands on this idea in a conversation with* **Joseph Horowitz**:

JH: The preludes. It seems to me that's the body of music by Chopin that most confounds the prejudices against him. Because you couldn't say that the preludes are *salon* music or a pretext for display. Do you always play them as a cycle?

CA: Yes. As a young man I would play them individually. But I stopped doing that — in the twenties, I think.

JH: Do you have individual favourites among the preludes?

CA: As I say, I never think of them as single pieces. They *answer* one another. When I finish one of them, I *need* to play the next. In a way, they are a survey of Chopin's cosmos. Alternating light and shade.

JH: I recently heard a tape of a performance you gave of the preludes in Los Angeles in 1969. And in some instances you went directly from one prelude to the next, without a break, without any silence in between. This doesn't occur on your recording, because the engineers have inserted bands.

CA: It reminds me a little bit of some of the connections between movements in late Beethoven. One movement *erupts,* in a completely different mood, out of the one before it. In Opus 109, for instance. Or Opus 101.

JH: Which preludes do you usually begin without an intervening silence?

CA: The B-flat minor [No. 16]. Also the D minor [No. 24].

JH: Could we go back to the First Prelude, and talk about some of the preludes individually?

CA: The First Prelude is definitely an introduction. An intensely dramatic introduction. It's over in half a minute or something. And it puts one in a certain tense emotional situation. It has something to do with sexual energy, this prelude. There's something positively orgasmic about it.

JH: The music heaves and heaves toward a climax.

CA: And that would explain the three bars with altered rhythm.

23

In these three bars, just before the climax, you don't breathe any more. The A-minor Prelude [No. 2] is fantastically desolate. But the next prelude, in G [No. 3], has something to do with a friendly landscape, or with spring.

JH: You make very much of the turn in the right hand [measure 17] — more, I think, than any other pianist I've heard. And you take a big rubato to make room for it.

CA: This is a period in which ornaments become part of the melodic line. Such ornaments should always be treated melodically in Chopin . . . The E minor Prelude [No. 4] is again melancholy. I can't think of any other music in which the melody is just two notes, and all the emotional events occur in the harmonic changes, shading the two notes with different colours and moods. And then when the espressivo phrases come in — because of the monotony of the two notes, they make an incredible impact.

JH: In the B minor Prelude [No. 6] you stress the two-note sighing inflections in the right hand, almost as a counter-subject to the melody in the left. Chopin is sometimes stigmatised as a one-handed composer. But I hear in your performances of a number of the preludes an unusual degree of individuality in both hands. In the G sharp minor Prelude [No. 12] your left hand has such amazing energy and definition that the prelude practically becomes a contest between the hands.

CA: You could say that the G minor Prelude [No. 22] is a struggle between the hands. The ending is fantastic. The left hand keeps insisting on the same thing, and the right hand, not knowing what to do, ascends to the utmost treble.

JH: I once heard you describe the E flat minor Prelude [No. 14] as the most 'enigmatic' in the cycle.

CA: The tempo is printed as largo in the Oxford edition, rather than allegro. That's why I pay it slowly. Chopin wrote it in with pencil or something. You know, it's sometimes interpreted in an impressionistic way. But to me this prelude is full of *Qual* — intense suffering. Exasperation.

JH: The E flat minor Prelude is often compared to the finale of the B flat minor Sonata, which is also written as two lines an octave apart.

CA: That finale has of course a lot to do with the 'Funeral March' movement that precedes it. They used to call it 'the wind over the grave'. The E flat minor Prelude, especially if you play it at the slower tempo, is more anguished.

JH: Another prelude that's enigmatic or elusive in somewhat the same way — because again there's no melody to speak of — is the F minor [No. 18].

CA: Oh yes. That's *tremendous.* There's a relationship between this and the second movement of the Beethoven G major Piano Concerto. It's again two conflicting elements. The upper voice is pleading in an absolutely *desperate* way. And the answering chords are a *furious* denial. The denial grows stronger and stronger. There is a terrific struggle. Here, unlike in the G major Concerto, there is no solution. The end is a collapse of the pleading voice. The final two chords are a rejection.

JH: Do you want to say anything about the last several preludes as a group — the way Chopin evolves toward a final statement? Is it fated, from the beginning, that the cycle will end so cataclysmically?

CA: No. Only after the B flat minor Prelude [No. 16], I would say, do you feel that his fundamental approach to life is tragic. The peaceful, positive preludes become like remembrances of the things that make life acceptable. Do you know Chopin's letter to his friend Titus [15, May 1830] about the second movement of the E minor Piano Concerto? About spring and the moonlight? The F major Prelude [No. 23] is very much like that. A bit *au bord d'une source.*

JH: Do you have trouble integrating the F major Prelude? Does it ever seem swallowed up by the G minor [No. 22] and D minor [No. 24]?

CA: No, no. It's absolutely necessary — this balancing, always showing the other side of life. If Chopin went directly from the G minor to the D minor Prelude, they would kill one another.

JH: And what about the D minor Prelude [No. 24]?

CA: There is a famous description of it — 'blood, voluptuousness, and death'. That says everything.

JH: You bring out the left hand very distinctly.

CA: I heard a performance the other day in which the left hand was a complete blur. But it is really a very dramatic element — like a stormy sea. You could say that the *plunge* at the end is like a drowning. Or that it cuts the thread of life — like the Fates in Greek mythology.

JH: What fingering do you use for the three final low Ds?

CA: Three-four-five. [Arrau forms a hard wedge with the last three fingers of his left hand.] That's absolutely sure. The possibility of hitting a wrong note doesn't exist, really. And it allows the transmission of the utmost power through the body.

JH: Why is your fingering better than using, say, the thumb, as Cortot recommends?

CA: With the thumb, you have to strike vertically or in a flat position. To strike vertically would be unavoidably hard and ugly. And with the flat position you are less sure of getting the amount of power you need.

JH: Are the preludes the darkest thing in Chopin?

CA: I would probably say yes. The ending is so *definite.* I mean, after this, you cannot find any great enthusiasm for life.

Conversations with Arrau

Turning from Arrau's comments on the Chopin Preludes to those of a great pianist one generation earlier, Alfred Cortot, one finds that though styles of expression have changed, the basic approach to interpretation has remained constant. Here are three examples for comparison:

No. 4 in E minor: *Largo*
Title suggested by Cortot: 'Beside a grave'
- **His remarks:** It would be hard to find in the whole melancholy and passionate production of the chosen poet of sorrow a more significant page than this one. It provides within the short span of its few bars one of the most poignant images of despair ever immortalized in music. Beneath the wailing insistence of the slow lament which the right hand wrings from the piano in long sobs, the left hand seems to remain frozen in the steady

27

indifference of monotonous and even chords. Note by note, the harmonies dissolve. An almost imperceptible descent leads to others still more affecting and more heart-rending; each of these changes, as though reopening a half-healed wound, suggests the renewal of an intolerable pain. The sad melody works itself up to a moment of frenzy which Chopin underlines only with the simple words *stretto* and *forte*. Then, broken, helpless and utterly exhausted by excessive grief, the melodic line doubles back on itself and is enclosed once more in the prostrate interval of a second which marks the whole of this Prelude. After a short and ominous silence, three muffled chords seem to invoke eternity from the edge of an open tomb . . . ideally, one should play this piece hiding one's tears in a veil of mourning. . . .

No. 14 in E flat minor: *Allegro*
Title suggested by Cortot: 'Stormy sea'
- **His remarks:** This Prelude has often been considered a sketch for the *Finale* of the *op. 35 Sonata,* that mysterious whirlwind fanned by the icy blasts of Death. Indeed the graphic lay-out is nearly the same . . . but while in the *Sonata* the pianist should try to give the melodic line an almost ghostlike and suspended quality, in these short and fierce bars, he should mainly underline the harmonic progressions and interpret the legato in the sense of weightiness.

No. 24 in D minor: *Allegro appassionato*
Title suggested in Cortot: 'Blood, passion and death'
- **His remarks:** The main obstacle to the playing of this most amazing product of Chopin's genius is the combination of the melodic element in the right hand, free, daring, passionate and proud, with the galloping *ostinato* figure in the left hand which retains throughout the same frightening uniformity, the rigidity of a stubborn rhythm . . . The *24th Prelude* overflows with emotion,

loaded with determination. Its dangerous incandescence requires the utmost mastery and control. In the frenzied gallop of the left hand, the bass note should always be sounded strongly. The pedal must be lifted all the way to emphasize the rhythm and to separate the two groups which form each bar. Do not play the scales as mere scales, but as flashes of lightning. . . .

Alfred Cortot
Taken from an EMI record sleeve

M. Frédéric Chopin has, by some means or other which we cannot divine, obtained an enormous reputation but too often refused to composers of ten times his genius. M. Chopin is by no means a putter-down of commonplaces; but he is, what by many would be esteemed worse, a dealer in the most absurd and hyperbolical extravagances. . . . The entire works of Chopin present a motley surface of ranting hyperbole and excruciating cacophony. When he is not *thus* singular, he is no better than Strauss or any other waltz-compounder. . . . There is an excuse at present for Chopin's delinquencies; he is entrammelled in the enthralling bonds of that arch-enchantress, George Sand, celebrated equally for the number and excellence of her romances and her lovers; not less we wonder how she, who once swayed the heart of the sublime and terrible religious democrat Lamennais, can be content to wanton away her dreamlike existence with an artistical nonentity like Chopin.

Musical World
London, 28 October 1841

A friendly applause greeted my appearance on the platform, and the orchestra rose to its feet. This made me feel so much better that I was now in the mood to do my best. But the Chopin concerto turned out to be a bad performance, by both the orchestra and myself. My usually good and full piano tone was lost on the unfamiliar and weak Gaveau concert grand, the delicate filigree of the larghetto was hardly audible, and in the third movement I actually stumbled once or twice. We received a polite applause; we didn't deserve better. Then came my solo pieces. The Brahms intermezzo, which I played quite well, was received with icy indifference. At that point I became desperate; I had prepared two Chopin études, the A flat, Opus 25 No. 1, and the No. 2, both beautiful but not very effective, so for this last one I substituted on the spur of the moment the grand Étude in A minor, Opus 25 No. 11, which was far from being ready for a performance. I banged out the heroic theme in the left hand with all my might, and smeared up, with the help of the pedal, the difficult passage work in the treble, and finished the piece in a brilliant flash! This provoked an ovation, even some 'Bravo' shouts from the gallery. I learned then, on the spot, that a loud, smashing performance, even the worst from a musical standpoint, will always get an enthusiastic reception by the uninitiated, unmusical part of the audience, and I exploited this knowledge, I admit it with shame, in many concerts to come.

Artur Rubinstein
My Young Years

Much of the emptiest and artistically most meaningless applause comes from the even worse habit of personality-worship. Indeed this amounts to a positive vice, which the lover of music cannot be strongly enough urged to shun. Although the cinema provides an excellent outlet for the shallowest seekers after entertainment, perhaps fortunately for music, there is no denying that the latter too suffers to some extent from the film-fan mentality of the less desirable of its patrons. There are people who will listen to anything from a prima donna who has to have half Scotland Yard on the stage of Covent Garden to watch her jewels, from a fiddler who has swum the Channel or from a pianist who has married first a peer and then a prize-fighter and is the mother of triplets. Beware of being caught by the glamour of such fascinating irrelevances.

Some newspapers, unfortunately, will do their best to spread what they call stories about an executive artist, particularly those who do not even pretend to take the slightest interest in their actual work. There are editors in Fleet Street who will welcome any indirect advertisement of an executive musician, provided only that it be sensational enough as news, while they will cut down the critic's notice of the same person's concert, supposing they do have a music critic at all and have not replaced him by a writer of musicians' gossip, to a minimum, if indeed he is lucky enough to escape having it reduced to nonsense for the sake of precious space, occupied more likely than not by the latest murder. Musical performers who are really anxious to endear themselves to the editors of the more popular and therefore presumably more useful Press might do worse than try their hands at some other than concert-room crimes. I would even go so far as to suggest to the most ardent seekers after notoriety among them that they might usefully put their own heads into the nearest gas ovens. To people who do not perform, but who wish to show a sensitive appreciation of the best performers I can only recommend that they should take no notice whatever of newspaper and other stories circulated about artists, but try them for what they are worth as musicians and form an independent judgement from that.

Eric Blom
An Essay on Performance and Listening

Arturo Benedetti Michelangeli

In 1939 at the first Geneva International Piano Competition a young man of 19 carried off the first prize having enthralled all the jury and the audience. This power to enthrall has never diminished, because the young man who was Arturo Benedetti Michelangeli occupies an exceptional place in the history of twentieth-century musical interpretation.

We know that he was born in Brescia on 5 January 1920. Legend has it that he is descended from St Francis of Assisi. Violinist, organist, doctor, Franciscan monk (he spent a year in a monastery), pilot, racing-car driver, first-class skier, piano technician — he is able to take a concert grand piano to pieces and reconstruct it — Arturo Benedetti Michelangeli is unique. If sometimes he is forced to disappoint his public by cancelling concerts, he has never disappointed the thousands who have heard him.

'He is Liszt reincarnated; he makes the piano more fluid,' exclaimed Alfred Cortot, whilst Maurice Ravel told him: 'You make my music sound more beautiful.'

He has a magnificent recording studio, where his pianos are thermostatically controlled at a constant temperature. He is nevertheless sorry that the pianos are not perfect: 'When will I have an instrument that works as well as a Ferrari?'

Music critics throughout the world have enthusiastically acclaimed his latest recordings, for all three of which he received the Edison Prize and *le Figaro* called him 'the pianist of the century'.

Royal Festival Hall Programme Note, mid-1970s
Author unknown

Michelangeli *is notorious for calling off his recitals with the minimum of notice or excuse. At the very recital from which that programme note was taken a lady with an enormous hat sat in the stalls of the packed hall and, to the request from* *those sitting behind her that she remove it, replied: 'Not until he's actually sitting at the piano!'*

Another pianist, **Adolf Henselt,** *also found public appearances a problem. His portrait is drawn by the music critic of the* New York Times, **Harold C. Schonberg,** *and I quote this at length (as I do from the same writer in the later section on conductors) because I find Schonberg's journalism irresistible.*

Adolf Henselt was terrified of the public, and it was a pathological terror. Once he was recognised in a café, and the band gave him an ovation. The horrified, suddenly galvanised Henselt blindly raced through the crowd and escaped through the kitchen. When playing with an orchestra he would hide in the wings until the opening tutti was over, rush out and literally pounce on the piano. On one occasion he forgot to put aside the cigar he was nervously chomping — this was in Russia — and played the concerto cigar in mouth, smoking away, much to the amusement of the Tsar. The mere thought of giving a concert made him physically ill. He gave very few throughout his career — far fewer than any of the great pianists, including Alkan — and in the last thirty-three years of his life apparently gave no more than three. (At least, that is what several reference books say.) He was offered fabulous sums to appear but turned down all offers. He just could not control his fingers when he knew people were listening.

All this may have come about because at his début, according to Alice Diehl, he had a memory lapse, left the stage and refused to return. He had been born in Bavaria and had studied with Hummel. Hummel thought him a young anarchist, and Henselt thought Hummel was an old fogy. When Henselt finally got enough nerve to appear in public he made an overwhelming impression. 'Liszt, Chopin and Henselt are continents; Tausig, Rubinstein and Bülow are countries.' Thus Wilhelm von Lenz. Liszt appears to have been amazed. 'Find

33

out the secret of Henselt's hands,' he told his pupils. 'I could have had velvet paws like that if I had wanted to.' Schumann wrote rave reviews, referring to Henselt as a mighty pianist who eclipsed everybody, 'who possesses the most equally developed hands, of iron strength and endurance, and capable of softness, grace and singing quality'. Henselt must have been able to draw a very penetrating tone from the piano. One of his pupils, Bettina Walker, tried to describe his touch, said it was hopeless to try, an absurd task, and then went on for a few hundred well-chosen words in which 'crystalline', 'sea', 'pearl', 'chalice', and 'flower' figure prominently. Pupils, of course, have a tendency to fall in love with their teachers, and their remarks are not to be taken too seriously. But Walker's remarks are echoed by too many good musicians for them to be unfounded.

The technical feature that Henselt had to an unprecedented degree was his amazing extensions. His hands were not particularly large; they were thick, fleshy, and had short fingers. But he worked so diligently on his extensions that he got to the point where his left-hand stretch could take in C-E-G-C-F and his right hand B-E-A-C-E. 'Leather! Just look how it is stretched,' he would say, displaying his palms. Such was the strength of his hands that he could get thunderous orchestral effects from his fingers alone, where Liszt had to work from the arms. Years and years of compulsive practice had brought him to the point where his fingers were absolutely independent, and musicians were entranced when he played Bach, bringing out the counterpoint with amazing clarity.

He may have been the most compulsive practiser in history — more, even, than Dreyschock, more than Godowsky. One reason for this concentration was that he was not a natural pianist, as Liszt was. He had to slave. By 1832 he got into the habit of working at the piano for ten hours a day, and he never let up. Even at the intermissions of his concerts, or on trains, or in stagecoaches, he would have a dummy keyboard on his knees. This kind of compulsive practice *could* not have meant much, if anything; it was merely relief from

34

tension, a kind of withdrawal, atonement for sin. One does not know whether to laugh or cry at von Lenz's description of Henselt at home:

> Such a study of Bach as Henselt made, every day of his life, has never before been heard of. He played the fugues most diligently on a piano so muffled with feather quills that the only sound heard was the dry beat of the hammers against the muffled strings; it was like the bones of a skeleton rattled by the wind! In this manner the great artist spared his ears and his nerves, for he reads, at the same time, on the music rack, a very thick, good book — the Bible — truly the most appropriate companion for Bach. After he has played Bach and the Bible quite through, he begins over again. The few people whom Henselt allows to approach him in those late, hallowed evening hours, he requests to continue their conversation — that does not disturb him in the least.

'At home' to Henselt was St Petersburg. He had gone there in 1838 and immediately been named court pianist, much to the despair of Charles Mayer. Mayer, a pianist with a good European reputation, had studied with Field in Russia and settled in St Petersburg. There he had played and taught — and had not once been asked to play at court. It was the only thing he wanted in life. Poor Mayer, broken-hearted, left St Petersburg and went to Dresden to die. Henselt replaced him as the pianistic celebrity, taught plentifully (including the royal family) and gave a series of matinées at court where, before a small audience, he could play at his best. He did not like audiences, but a small one, mostly of friends, was preferable to a big one.

Henselt was a textbook German, relentless to the point of savagery as a teacher (he obviously detested teaching), and he was equally arrogant in his musical *obiter dicta.* Certain modernistic things in music he never understood, and the dissonant chord that opens the last movement of the Beethoven Ninth he referred to as 'a monster'. To illustrate this chord he would turn his back to the piano, sit on the keys and say, 'It sounds something like this.' His teaching sessions were on the spectacular side. Students would enter all atremble to be greeted by a Henselt dressed in a white suit, wearing a red fez, clutching a fly-swatter in his hands. 'Begin!' The pupil would begin and soon hit a wrong note. '*Falsch!* Play it again!' So went the lesson. '*Falsch! Falsch!*' In the meantime he was striding around the room, swatting flies. If he were completely uninterested in the pupil he would stop trying to decimate the fly population of Russia, bring in his dogs and play with them. Small wonder that he never turned out an important pupil. Students who did interest him received fairer treatment, including much illustration at the second piano; but Henselt was notoriously short-tempered and few seemed to interest him. Those few came away with their spirit broken. He worked them to death, and assured them that they had no talent. There was a saying in pianistic circles: 'Henselt kills.'

Harold C. Schonberg
The Great Pianists

From *Evenings in the Orchestra* by Hector Berlioz:

Tuesday, 22 July
The Conservatoire competitions started last week. On the opening day M. Auber resolves to take the bull by the horns, as they say, and to make the pianists compete first. The intrepid jury appointed to hear the candidates is apparently undismayed at the news that there are thirty-one of them, eighteen women and thirteen men. The work prescribed for the competition is Mendelssohn's G minor Concerto. Unless an

36

apoplectic fit strikes down one of the candidates during the session, the concerto will therefore have thirty-one consecutive performances; that much is known. But there are other facts you may not yet know, and which I had not heard myself a few hours ago, having cautiously avoided this experiment. They were related to me this morning by one of the Conservatoire attendants as I was crossing the courtyard of that establishment, my mind full of the ageing epithet which the Amaryllis of Montmorency had conferred upon me.

'Oh, poor M. Érard,' he was saying, 'what a calamity!'

'What's happened to Érard?'

'D'you mean to say that you weren't at the piano competition?'

'No, I most certainly wasn't. Well, what happened?'

'Just imagine, M. Érard was kind enough to lend us, for that day, a magnificent piano which he had just finished and which he was planning to send to London for the 1851 Great Exhibition. That shows you how proud he was of it. It had a deafening sonority, a bass such as you never heard in your life before, it was altogether an extraordinary instrument. The keys were just slightly stiff; but that's why he'd sent it to us. M. Érard is no fool, and he'd said to himself: 'The thirty-one pupils, by dint of banging away at their concerto, will liven up the keys of my piano and this will be all to the good.' Yes indeed, but the poor man didn't foresee that his keyboard would be livened up in such a terrible fashion. Just think, a concerto performed thirty-one times running in a single day! Who could prophesy the results of such repetition? The first pupil duly appears and, finding the piano a trifle stiff, hammers on the sound lustily. The second, *idem.* At the third assault, the piano already offers less resistance; it resists still less at the fifth. I don't know how the sixth competitor found it; just as he came on, I had to fetch a bottle of ether for one of the gentlemen of the jury, who was feeling faint. The seventh was just finishing when I got back, and I heard him say as he walked off: 'That piano isn't as stiff as they make out; on the contrary, I think it's excellent.' The next ten or twelve competitors agreed with him; the last of them even insisted that, far from being too stiff to the touch, it was too loose.

'At about a quarter to three, we'd reached number twenty-six, after starting at ten o'clock. It was Mlle Hermance-Lévy's turn. The conditions could not have been more favourable for her, since she hates stiff pianos, and everybody was now complaining that the slightest pressure on the key-board made it sound. And so she dashed off the concerto so lightly that she won the first prize outright. When I say out-right, I'm not being quite accurate; she shared it with Mlle Vidal and Mlle Roux. These two young ladies also took advantage of the looseness of the keyboard, which was now so extreme that the keys moved if one so much as breathed on them. Who ever saw a piano like this? Just as we were going to hear number twenty-nine, I had to go out again to fetch a doctor; another of the gentlemen of the jury was growing crimson in the face, and had to be bled urgently. Oh, the piano competition is no joke! And when the doctor arrived, he was not a moment too soon. As I was returning to the theatre foyer, I saw number twenty-nine leaving the stage. It was the young Planté, deadly pale, and trembling from head to foot. He was saying, 'I don't know what's wrong with the piano, but the keys move of their own accord. It's as though there were somebody inside pushing the hammers. I'm frightened.' 'Come off it, youngster, you're imagining things,' replies young Cohen, who is three years his senior. 'Let me by; I'm not afraid.' Cohen (number thirty) goes on; he sits down at the piano without looking at the keyboard, plays his concerto very well, and after the last chord, just as he was getting up — believe it or not, the piano starts playing the concerto again all by itself! The poor young man, for all his bragging, remained as though petrified for a second, and then took to his heels. From that moment, the piano plays away more and more loudly, tossing off scales, trills, and arpeggios. The public, seeing nobody near the instrument, yet hearing it sound with ten times its former volume, starts to fidget

38

throughout the theatre. Some people laugh, others are growing frightened, all are filled with understandable amazement. There was just one juryman who couldn't see the stage from the back of his box. Thinking that M. Cohen had started the concerto again, he was shouting himself hoarse: 'Enough! Enough! Enough! Shut up, will you! Call the last competitor, number thirty-one.' We had to call to him from the theatre: 'Sir, nobody's playing; it's the piano that's got so used to the Mendelssohn concerto that it's giving it's own version of it, all by itself. Take a look.' 'Well I never! It's all highly improper. Call M. Érard. Bustle up; he'll perhaps manage to bring that abominable instrument under control.' We go to fetch M. Érard. Meanwhile the rascally piano, which had finished its concerto, relentlessly started it again without losing a single moment. The din grew and grew until it seemed as though four dozen pianos were playing in unison. There were runs, tremolos, scales in sixths and thirds repeated at octave intervals, ten-note chords, triple trills, a deluge of sounds, the loud pedal, the whole confounded works.

'M. Érard arrives; despite his efforts, the piano, which no longer knows itself, doesn't know its master either. He sends for holy water, he sprinkles the keyboard, but to no effect: a proof that this was no spell, but the natural result of the thirty performances of the same concerto. They take the instrument to pieces, and remove the keyboard which is still moving. They throw it into the courtyard of the state repository where M. Érard, in his fury, has it chopped to pieces. But blow me if this didn't make matters worse! All the pieces danced and leapt about, frisked in different directions, over the cobbles, between our legs, up against the wall, everywhere — until finally the repository locksmith picked up all these fragments of bewitched mechanism in a single armful and threw them into the fire in his forge so as to dispose of them once and for all. Poor M. Érard! Such a fine instrument, too! We were all heartbroken. But what else could be done? This was the only way of getting rid of it. After playing a single concerto thirty times running in the same hall on the same day, it's no wonder, after all, if the piano gets into a rut! Of course M. Mendelssohn won't be able to complain that his music isn't played! But look at the result!'

I shall not add anything to the account which you have just read, and which has all the appearances of a fantastic tale. No doubt you will not believe a word of it, you will go as far as to say: 'It's absurd.' But it is because of its very absurdity that I believe it, for a Conservatoire attendant would never have invented such an extravagant story.

In my twenty-five odd years of broadcasting experience it has never failed to astonish me that, no matter what you say (and I really mean no matter what) there will always be someone who agrees with you and someone who doesn't. State what you think to be a self-evident truth: 'The three greatest composers who have ever lived are Bach, Mozart and Beethoven', and you will receive a reproachful letter from The Friends of Johannes Brahms. Dismiss the entire output of Verdi as 'the ravings of an organ grinder', and someone will write you a glowing testimonial, praising you for having the courage to expose the old Italian fraud.

It is, therefore, both safe and dangerous to say anything, even if you are a composer of the stature of **Paul Hindemith**.

From *The Language of Music* by Deryck Cooke:

Again, we may note how the tragic subjects of the St Matthew

Passion and *Die Winterreise* forced on Bach and Schubert a heavy (almost too heavy) preponderance of minor keys; while the brighter subjects of the Easter Oratorio and most of *Die schöne Müllerin* turned them inevitably towards the major. Did anyone ever set the Resurrexit of the Mass to slow, soft, minor music? Or the Crucifixus to quick, loud, major strains? Try singing the word 'Crucifixus' to the music of Handel's Hallelujah Chorus, or the word 'Hallelujah' to the music of the Crucifixus in Bach's B minor Mass! Stravinsky himself has complied with the common practice in these matters. In the *Symphony of Psalms,* the first two movements (settings of sombre prayer-psalms) are in E minor and C minor respectively, while the last (a setting of a praise-psalm) moves between E flat major and C major. And his *Oedipus Rex* is mainly in minor keys, his *Rake's Progress* mainly in major ones. Within the orbit of tonality, composers have always been bound by certain expressive laws of the medium, laws which are analogous to those of language.

So we must admit that composers have set out to express emotion, and that listeners have felt it to be present in their music. But we must still consider Stravinsky's opinion that, 'if, as is nearly always the case, music appears to express something, this is only an illusion, and not a reality'.

This point of view has been set forth in greater detail by Hindemith in his book *A Composer's World.* His theory is that music does have an emotive effect on the listener, but the apparent emotions are not those of the composer, nor do they arouse the real emotions of the listener; in Stravinsky's words 'this is only an illusion'. Hindemith says: 'Music cannot express the composer's feelings. Let us suppose a composer is writing an extremely funereal piece, which may require three months of intensive work. Is he, during this three-month period, thinking of nothing but funerals? Or can he, in those hours that are not devoted to his work because of his desire to eat and sleep, put his grief on ice, so to speak, and be gay until the moment when he resumes his sombre activity? If he really expressed his feelings accurately during the time of composing and writing, we would be presented with a horrible motley of expressions, among which the grievous part would necessarily occupy but a small space.' Later, he continues: 'If the composer himself thinks he is expressing his own feelings, we have to accuse him of lack of observation. Here is what he really does: he knows by experience that certain patterns of tone-setting correspond with certain emotional reactions on the listener's part. Writing these patterns frequently and finding his observations confirmed, in anticipating the listener's reaction he believes himself to be in the same mental situation.'

The *naïveté* and illogicality of this analysis, coming from a composer of Hindemith's mental stature, is truly regrettable. But we have to remember again that composers write out of their own experience; and we know that Hindemith is, and sees himself as, a superior kind of craftsman, not an 'inspired genius' — that, in fact, he rather derisively denies the existence of inspiration: 'Melodies can, in our time, be constructed rationally. We do not need to believe in benign fairies, bestowing angelic tunes upon their favourites.' Being this kind of a composer, he is unable, despite his intellectual insight into musical construction and his laudable concern for music's moral values, to understand the deep unconscious urges that gave birth to music of the deeply emotive kind — viz., most of the music written between 1400 and the present day.

There seems to be in Hindemith's analysis an almost wilful refusal to understand that an artist has two separate selves: the everyday, conscious self, which is a prey to many passing trivial emotions, and a deep, unconscious, creative self, which is always there to return to, 'inspiration' permitting, and which is apt to intrude itself intermittently, as 'inspiration', during his everyday life. If Hindemith has no personal experience of this, surely he has heard of the fits of 'absent-mindedness' that some great artists have been subject to, when this occurred? Surely he must have some conception of the way in which this unconscious creative self persists beneath the distractions of everyday life, concentrated on its all-important realities? When we state that a composer, writing a

42

lengthy piece over a long period, expresses his emotions in it, we really ought not to have to explain that we mean his deep, permanent, significant emotions, not the superficial fleeting ones called forth by trivial pleasures and disappointments.

What a composer feels (or doesn't feel) when writing music is, of course, a huge area for debate, so I shall avoid it (for the time being) and return to the piano.

In his book Chopin Playing — From the Composer to the Present Day **James Methuen-Campbell** *chose to question the validity of paraphrases of the composer's works made by the Polish pianist* **Leopold Godowsky**, *but although Godowsky died in 1938 there still exists a Godowsky Society which is very much alive, corresponding regularly, and in daunting detail, and ever watchful for the good name of the master.*

The mention of Mr James Methuen-Campbell brings me to his fascinating book *Chopin Playing — From the Composer to the Present Day* . . . a rivetingly readable book, indispensable, as the blurb states, to all who are interested in the piano. One of the pleasures of this book is that there is much to disagree with. However, and I do not write this *just* because of my devotion to Godowsky, there is something in it that I must take issue with, and that is, of course, the portion relating to Godowsky. After a brief biographical sketch, Mr Methuen-Campbell writes:

> Early in his carrer, Godowsky caught the disease of transcribing and adapting the music of other composers, Chopin in particular. A master of contrapuntal writing, he used all his skill to introduce new melodic lines, rewrite parts and 'touch up' original compositions in a manner which, although intricate and fascinating, must of course be challenged on musical grounds. He was

43

fond of the two Chopin Concertos, for which he rewrote the orchestral and solo parts. In the F minor Concerto, he introduced counter-melodies for the left hand in contrast with the right, thus wrecking Chopin's original intention. He rewrote the twenty-seven études, producing over fifty new creations which include studies for the left hand alone, two études combined together, and many tortuous exercises which take instrumental writing to the heights of complexity.

This seems to indicate that the author suffers from the modern disease of 'good taste', as well as sounding like received opinion. The art of transcription has been practised by reliable practitioners of music from Bach to Stravinsky. It also shows a melancholy misunderstanding of Godowsky's purpose in writing his studies, which is a sad blemish on a deeply researched book as it indicates a complete ignorance of this work of Godowsky's which a reading of the three-part exposition to the collected *Studies* would have clarified.

Harry Winstanley
The Godowsky Society Newsletter, No. 11 Vol. 2

Mr Methuen-Campbell's painstakingly researched and comprehensive book lists virtually every professional pianist in history who has set finger to a polonaise or mazurka, and the sad truth is that the more generous his scope, the more liable he is to be attacked. So now, like a shark smelling blood in the water, I too will swim up for a bite.
Here is part of the chapter on one of my particular heroes, the Rumanian pianist **Dinu Lipatti:**

Although Lipatti's discs are very few, several of them are of

Chopin's music, of which he was a supreme interpreter. The major recordings of Chopin that we have are of the B minor Sonata (1947), the E minor Concerto (1948, with an unnamed, though very distinguished, orchestra), the fourteen waltzes (1949), the Barcarolle (1948), and the waltzes again (thirteen this time, from the Besançon Festival of 1950, recorded when the artist had only a few months to live). The E minor Concerto and the thirteen waltzes come from public concerts. Most of the discs represent his playing with great fidelity, since he was a pianist who always gave of his best.

Lipatti's interpretations were startlingly convincing. In the E minor Concerto, one is aware from the first piano entry of being in the presence of a persuasive force — Lipatti's sound world has a magical quality, full of thought and dedication, which entirely captivates the listener. He resembled Cortot in his grasp of the composer's idiom, but he did not possess his teacher's very distinctive rubato, nor quite the same monumental stature. Lipatti was able to play Chopin's best-known works and make them sound as if he was performing them for the first time, whereas Cortot's playing conveys the sense that he had absorbed the music into his blood and played from a wealth of experience. Lipatti's playing had the clarity and precision of the French school, combined with a greater imagination and greater inner freedom than most French pianists possess. His mood in this concerto is in general one of gentle persuasion, though the variety of his approach is shown by the coda of the first movement, which has an alarming menace, the desperate wildness also heard on Rosenthal's version.

Unfortunately, on 5 August 1981 (the year that the book was published) the record company, EMI, had a confession to make concerning the performance of the E minor Concerto which had given Mr Methuen-Campbell such pleasure, and on which he had written with such insight.

In 1965 a tape of this concerto came to the attention of his widow, Mme Lipatti. Not only did she identify it as being of her husband, but also Walter Legge who, as his producer, was personally responsible for securing for posterity such few recordings as survive. Ernest Ansermet, the great Swiss conductor, also identified the performance as unquestionably by Lipatti. With such authoritative authentication EMI issued the recording, first in the USA on Seraphim in 1965 and subsequently in many other countries. As it could never be established which conductor and orchestra were accompanying Lipatti, EMI paid to the Swiss Musicians' Union a sum of money to be claimed if ever the correct accompaniment was identified.

Seventeen years later, when EMI Records reissued the recording as part of the set entitled 'The Art of Dinu Lipatti', the BBC broadcast the concerto again. A listener wrote to the BBC* claiming that the recording was identical with a Supraphon recording, first published in the early 1950s, of the distinguished Polish pianist Halina Czerny-Stefanska.

Both the BBC* and the International Classical Division of EMI have now tested the recordings and found them to be absolutely identical.

In plain language, the recording is not by Lipatti at all!

I became involved in that minor controversy because, as I said earlier, Dinu Lipatti holds a very special place in my heart. If you have been lucky enough to hear him play, or listened to his records, you will know why. If not, then I hope the following two pieces will help to convey something of his genius.

*The first was written by the distinguished executive producer at Columbia Records, **Walter Legge**, and published in* Gramophone *Magazine two months after Lipatti's*

*Just for the record, it was me in both cases.

tragically early death.

The second, by his widow **Madeleine Lipatti,** *is taken from the sleeve which encloses the records of his last recital.*

Dinu Lipatti had the qualities of a saint. The spiritual goodness of his nature, his modesty, his gentleness, his will's firm purpose, his nobility and loftiness of thought and action communicated themselves to all who met him, and to the remotest listeners in the halls where he played. His goodness and generosity evoked faith, hope and charity in those around him. We not only hoped — we had faith. Even his doctors believed that the incurable disease he had suffered for six years would miraculously yield to some hitherto untried treatment, or that some new cure would be discovered before it was too late. Last June and July we had reason to believe that this miracle had happened. Injections of cortisone, the American preparation which at the time had spectacular successes in the treatment of rheumatoid arthritis, arrested his malady's progress and gave him a brief summer of well-being, high spirits and energy. This treatment was expensive — the injections cost $50 a day — but as soon as the facts became known musicians like Charles Munch and Yehudi Menuhin, as well as private persons, many of them anonymous Swiss admirers, guaranteed him several months' supply. He was the cause of goodness in others. But cortisone was only a dam, not a remedy. When the injections ceased the disease resumed its inexorable course. The inevitable end came on the afternoon of 2 December. He was 33.

Lipatti was born in Bucharest (19 March 1917) and cradled in music. His father was a wealthy amateur who had studied with Sarasate and Carl Flesch; his mother was a good pianist; Georges Enesco was his godfather. Music was his preoccupation from infancy. His mother has told me that he could play the piano before he had learned to smile. At four he gave concerts for charity and began composing pieces describing the characters of his family and their friends. It was never in question that he should devote his life to music, but only later

47

did circumstances dictate that he should become a professional pianist. He never attended school: professors from the University of Bucharest tutored him at home, building his general education around his music. His pianoforte teacher was a woman, Florica Musicesco. In winters in Bucharest and in summers on the family estate at Fonda she stood over the boy, relentlessly building that incomparable technique and magical touch. Admitted early by special dispensation he entered the Conservatoire before he was old enough officially to take the entrance examination. In 1933 he entered for the International Competition in Vienna. At the stormy final session Constantin (his baptismal name, Dinu is a diminutive) Lipatti was awarded second prize, and Alfred Cortot resigned from the jury as a protest that Lipatti had not been given the first prize. Before he left Vienna Cortot invited Lipatti to Paris to study with him.

In Paris he worked at pianoforte with Cortot and studied conducting with Charles Munch. On the evidence of some compositions submitted to the Conservatoire Paul Dukas had accepted him as a pupil with the comment: 'We have nothing to teach him; all we can do is encourage him to compose and guide his development.' Dukas died shortly afterwards and Lipatti was put under the care of Nadia Boulanger, who at once became, in Ansermet's words, 'his spiritual mother'. That noble and energetic woman, who has been the artistic conscience and guide to three decades of musical life in Paris, remained a close friend to the end of his life and a powerful influence on him. It was Nadia Boulanger who first brought him to recording. In 1937 he recorded with her and four singers Brahms's Liebeslieder Waltzes and a selection of Brahms's other waltzes.

In 1936 Lipatti began to make his name as a pianist with concerts in Berlin and various Italian cities. At the outbreak of war he returned to Rumania, where he stayed until 1943 when, together with his fiancée, Madeleine Cantacuzene, he escaped from Bucharest, and by devious ruses and routes they arrived, via Stockholm, in Geneva with a joint capital of five Swiss francs. The fates and the Genevese were kind. He was offered the post of professor of the virtuoso class at the Geneva Conservatory. His reputation as an artist and teacher spread rapidly. In Paris, in 1944, Francis Poulenc told me of 'this artist of divine spirituality', a judgement I was fully to endorse a few months later at a rehearsal of Chopin's F minor Concerto. From January 1946, Lipatti had an exclusive recording contract with English Columbia.

He was already an ill man. Frail from childhood, the illness which was eventually to destroy him had taken its hold. From 1948 onwards his fame was such that he could command his own terms to play whatever he chose. Tours in North and South America, and in Australia, which would have provided him with the money he so badly needed, were arranged and at the last minute cancelled on doctor's orders, but his complaint was for the inconvenience and expense that he had caused others.

Our first recordings were ill-starred. In July 1946 he made a series of records in Zürich which, owing to an unforeseen fault in the material, were not good enough for publication. After that unfortunate start all his recordings, except his last incredible achievements of July 1950, were made in the Abbey Road Studios, in London. Only his illness is to blame for the comparatively small number of records he made.

In the last days of May 1950 I had a private letter from a Dr Dubois-Ferrière in Geneva urging me at once to organise an expedition to Geneva to record Dinu Lipatti. As his doctor he had administered injections of cortisone and the improvement was remarkable.

Unfortunately, he explained, the treatment could not be continued for more than two months, and since this was the first time it had been tried for Lipatti's complaint he could give no promise of its permanence or continued efficacy, but he begged me as a friend of Lipatti's to stop at nothing to make recordings in Geneva possible while the improvement lasted. I found Dinu in better health and spirits than I had ever known him to enjoy. Friends had placed at his disposal a

49

house standing in its own small park, outside Geneva and a few minutes' walk from the French frontier. We christened it 'Haus Triebschenli', because it looked like a diminutive copy of Wagner's house on Lake Lucerne. Dinu loved the sun and the trees, and the weather smiled on us. For two radiant and blessed weeks the sun shone out of a clear blue sky and the thermometer settled itself comfortably in the nineties. Cortisone had given him a ravenous appetite and restored his natural gaiety. Dinu laughed and made music. He had just heard the story of Furtwängler, known among musicians for his nervous and seemingly undecided downbeat who, at the beginning of his first rehearsal of *Das Rheingold* with La Scala Orchestra had been encouraged by a shout from the first contra-bass player: 'Coraggio! Maestro, coraggio!' Whenever an arpeggio in the Chopin valses failed to come off with the desired clarity, accuracy and grace, Dinu stopped and called out either in apology or impatience: 'Arpeggio Maestro! Arpeggio.' It became a catch phrase which he cherished to the end. And when a legato passage was less smooth or chords less brilliant than he wanted it was always: *'Doigts de Macaroni'* — macaroni fingers — the contemptuous epithet which he used on himself and his pupils for a lack of controlled strength in the fingers. . . .

Madeleine, his wife, was invaluable and [an] incomparable collaborator. A pupil of the same teacher and herself a magnificent pianist and teacher — I doubt if she has her equal in the latter field — she hears and senses overtones and subtleties of nuance with ears that matched, and might have been, his. Her art, as well as her love and selflessness, are also in Dinu Lipatti's work. . . . Dinu played only twice in public after those July recordings. Mozart's C major Concerto with Herbert von Karajan at the Lucerne Festival and the recital at the Besançon Festival which these records fortunately immortalise. I do not believe that there has been, or will be, a pianist like Dinu Lipatti. It is not a matter of comparisons of quality, it is a matter of difference in kind. Hard as he worked and thought on purely technical problems of touch, sonority and pedalling, he was not a 'virtuoso' in the word's modern
50

and debased sense — but certainly in its seventeenth-century application 'a connoisseur'. For himself he had no use for display or brilliance of execution as ends in themselves, though he was almost over-generous in his praise and admiration for his contemporaries who have. He was a musician, a musician who used the pianoforte as a means of communication and expression. Only in terms of his qualities as a musician and a man can one hope to explain, to understand or describe him.

He was a good man in the highest sense, and a particularly sensitive one. He was in all things an aristocrat of the finest fibre, temperamentally incapable of vulgarity in thought or deed. He was fastidious and distinguished in all he did, unable, in showing a pupil how *not* to phrase, even of imitating bad taste. When he played jazz to amuse his friends or shock the seriousness out of some too earnest guest, he could not avoid giving the most trivial tune the lustre of his magical sound and delicate sensibility. He approached music with a composer's mind and his love for his favourite masters was blended with reverence. When I first knew him he had never played Beethoven: he felt he was not yet worthy. That he played the 'Waldstein' Sonata in the last two years of his life was due to the encouragement of Artur Schnabel who, as a wise and paternal admirer, persuaded him to take the plunge.

Lipatti's sense of responsibility to the public came out of his reverence for music. In the five years we worked together I was able to offer him a repertoire for recording for which many another pianist would have sacrificed his wife and family. Lipatti was not to be deflected from his devoted approach. To prepare the 'Emperor' Concerto he would need four years, even for the Tchaikovsky he needed three. Nothing in his work was unprepared or left to chance. He had his schedule of works to be studied and practised carefully mapped out for five years in advance. He never played a note in public that was not meticulously prepared: his miraculous playing was the result of a mastery of the physical-technical part of his art, so complete that his mind and spirit were free to express themselves in music.

51

The softness of his sound came through strength. He had enormous and powerful hands — the 'little' finger as long as its neighbour — and the shoulders of a wrestler, quite disproportionate to his frail build. As he played, each finger had a life and personality of its own, independent of its neighbours, of his wrists and arms: each finger seemed prehensile and the ten of them, when he played contrapuntal music, looked like a fantastic ballet danced by ten elephants' trunks each obeying the order of its own mahout. This visual impression of each finger having its own life is evident in the sound of his playing. Every note he played had a life of its own. To his pupils and to himself he preached giving every phrase and every note in every phrase 'character'. Every note in every part must live and contribute its meaning to the whole. He aimed at presenting the music of other periods in such a way that it would have for us today the vitality and significance it had had for the composer and his contemporaries. He did not seek in Bach to imitate the sound of a cembalo or clavier, he set out to play it as he believed Bach would have done if he had had a modern concert grand at his disposal. For this reason he occasionally and discreetly added octaves or transposed the lower voice down an octave. In certain works of Liszt he used the modern resources of pedalling to obtain effects implicit in the character of the music, but beyond the resources of Liszt's instruments. These were the only liberties he allowed himself or his pupils, who adored him.

Half an hour before he died he was listening to records of Beethoven's F minor Quartet. To his wife he said: 'You see, it is not enough to be a great composer. To write music like that you must be a chosen instrument of God.' By the same light we may say that it is not enough to be a great pianist: to play as Lipatti played you must be a chosen instrument of God.

God lent the world His chosen instrument whom we called Dinu Lipatti for too brief a space.

Walter Legge
Gramophone, February 1951

The particularly touching nature of this recording can leave no one unmoved. It was made at Besançon, on 16 September 1950 at Dinu Lipatti's last concert: the end-point of a career that was glorious despite its brevity. He was to die two months later, on 2 December at the age of 33.

Although very ill, he wanted to keep his promise, this engagement to play at Besançon. His doctors tried to dissuade him, but in vain, so absolute was Lipatti's determination not to 'betray'.

For him a concert was a pledge of his love to music, which he considered to be a 'serious thing' and also the desire, through the music, to give joy to those who always flocked to hear him.

He arrived at Besançon on the eve of the concert in a state of such grave weakness that it was only with difficulty that he could go to Parliament Hall, where the concert was to take place, in order to 'try' the piano. Back at the hotel, his attacks increased to the point where that faithful friend, his doctor, who had accompanied him, tried again to dissuade him. But Lipatti kept obstinately repeating, 'I promised; I *must* play!'

He was given numerous injections to revive him and, like an automaton, he dressed and slowly made his way to the car that was to take him to the hall. Once there, it was a real Calvary for him to climb the stairs, for he could not breathe; one could sense that he was close to fainting.

Outbursts of applause greeted his arrival in the hall. The audience, which had come from everywhere, was overwhelmed with emotion; it was there to hear for the last time this young genius who was — it knew — about to die.

We are now able to judge, thanks to this recording, the quality of his playing, the integrity of his thought, the validity of his interpretation. Only one moment of weakness, but how moving a one: he no longer had the strength to play the last of the fourteen waltzes. But we know that even Chopin would not have held it against him. . . .

Broken by fatigue, scarcely breathing, Lipatti yet had the courage to play that Bach chorale which, for him, was a prayer.

53

No one who was present at that concert will ever be able to forget that heartrending farewell; but, 'like those extinguished stars whose fire still gives us light', the art of Lipatti remains living in our hearts. Its message is a lesson, a joy that lasts.

Madeleine Lipatti
Geneva, 2 February 1957

Of all the many records on my shelves, those of Lipatti are the last I would be parted from.

I think I have learned at least 50 per cent, possibly more, of what I know about music from gramophone records, and in the process I have become something of a connoisseur on the subject of sleeve-note writing. In the main it is a thankless, poorly paid task and by no means easy to do well. So, as we move from pianists to pictures, I offer next one of the most concise and elegant examples of the form in my possession. It is taken from the sleeve of an EMI record of Richard Rodney Bennett's music for the film Lady Caroline Lamb *and I suppose we should expect it to be good, for it is written by one of our finest playwrights, the author, and director of the film,* Robert Bolt.

Lady Caroline, darling of the House of Devonshire, was by turns delightful and impossible. She was delicate and daring,
54

naïve and witty, fey, unstable, extreme in everything. She was not cut out for marriage but she wished to marry William Lamb. And to do what she wished was her only fixed principle — for Caroline was a romantic.

William was a Melbourne, and the Melbourne mode was classical. Caroline was fascinated by his poise and he by her extravagance. It was a marvellous union of opposite natures and while it went well it went very well indeed. But when it went badly it went with a bang.

The poet Byron was romance personified. The best and worst in Caroline responded to the best and worst in him. Their *affaire* was sensational, absurd. She did not mind absurdity. But in him there was a streak of something classical, something cynical and worldly which she minded very much. He cooled towards her and she became desperate. He savagely and publicly rejected her and she went half mad.

Now William gave up his brilliant political career and tried to nurse her back to happiness and health. And Caroline tried to respond. They loved each other more at this than any other time. But it was a wistful and autumnal love. There was too much sacrifice and effort in it. Nor could their natures change — Caroline's attempts to rehabilitate herself in Good Society were bizarre and ruinous.

They were still young when they agreed to part; the parting killed her. Hostility and ridicule she could sustain, not loneliness and disregard.

William lived on to be old but he never forgot her and never found a substitute. He lived alone into another age, that vulgarly romantic age which gave birth to our own. He was the first of Victoria's Prime Ministers and last of the Regency bucks.

The virtues and vices of the two great modes are most apparent in music. Romantic music at its best invokes and deepens our emotion, at worst invokes and cheapens it. Classical music at its best invokes emotion but contains it, at its worst is merely polite. I thought at first to have a classical theme for William, a romantic theme for Caroline. But Richard

55

Rodney Bennett pointed out that this would pull the story into its component parts instead of binding it together. He also told me that, like it or lump it, the tale I had told was a thoroughly romantic one, and only its framing and background were classical. The music he wrote is quite magically emotional — I find it so at any rate — yet beautifully well-mannered, the best of both worlds.

Films are fantasy and fantasy needs music.

Jack L. Warner
New York Times, 28 March 1976

During the making of *Lifeboat* at Twentieth Century-Fox in 1944, composer David Raksin was stopped in the studio commissary by a friend and told, perhaps a little too pointedly, that Alfred Hitchcock had decided against using any music in the score of the film. Raksin, inured to snide comments on film music, mused for a moment and asked why and how that unusual decision had been reached. Said the friend, 'Well, Hitchcock feels that since the entire action of the film takes place in a lifeboat on the open ocean, where would the music come from?' Replied Raksin, 'Ask Mr Hitchcock to explain where the cameras come from, and I'll tell him where the music comes from.'

Amusing though it may be, this anecdote puts its finger on a sore spot — the general lack of understanding about the role of music in films. It is a role that is not even fully understood in the film industry itself, possibly because music is the most abstract of the film arts as well as being the most abused and the most exploited. Famous producers and directors have been heard to say that if pictures were better made they wouldn't need music, to which the composers reply — good

56

pictures are made by the presence of talent, not the lack of music.

Film composers operate on strange terms. A good score can't save a bad film and a bad score can't kill a good picture. There is a certain stigma to film music and it is partly warranted by the large amount of appalling material that has been written over the years. Ironically, the general level of film music is not alone the responsibility of composers. The composer is a hired man — he works for a producer. Unfortunately, far too many producers have tin ears to match their itching palms and in craving only the most obviously commercial music for their films, they are rather like the man who would march into Tiffany's and say, 'Show me what you have in chrome.'

A chilling example of musical ignorance on a high level occurred during the completion of *The Battle of Britain*. Sir William Walton was hired to score the film, a logical choice, not only in view of his skill but the fact that his soaring music for *Spitfire/First of the Few* in 1942 is a highlight in the annals of film music. After Walton's score for *The Battle of Britain* had been recorded, the tapes were flown to New York. There a high-ranking officer of United Artists, who deserves the distinction of being anonymous, listened and said, 'The music stinks, get somebody else.' A lighter-weight composer, Ron Goodwin, who had written an agreeable score for *Those Magnificent Men in Their Flying Machines,* was brought in and wrote a competent, straightforward score. Goodwin is an undeniably tuneful composer, and he was probably somewhat embarrassed over the Walton matter. But a job is a job — particularly the job of scoring a multi-million-dollar picture. On hearing about this dumping of his friend Walton's score, Sir Laurence Olivier made it known to the producers that he would have his name removed from the credits unless some part of the Walton score was retained. This would have been an ugly bit of publicity since Olivier's role as Air Marshal Dowding was the most crucial one in the film. The producers decided to keep Sir William's scoring for the five-minute segment towards the end of the film in which a montage of aerial dog-fights are presented minus the sounds of the planes and almost like a surrealist ballet. Beautifully photographed, this sequence, dramatically and eerily scored by Walton, is easily the highlight of a generally disappointing film.

Tony Thomas
Music for the Movies

The conflict between the producer of a motion picture and the composer of the incidental music is further highlighted by the following two extracts from the memos of Hollywood Titan **David O. Selznick.**

The first, to fellow-executive Katharine Brown, of 30 August 1934, begins reasonably enough. Indeed one is most sympathetic to the opening two paragraphs, but the third sounds a warning bell, and the last is positively depressing.

TO: MISS KATHARINE BROWN

Answering your questions, and so that you will know about these matters for the future, the usual method of scoring pictures is for the arranger and scorer not to come near the picture until the editing is completed. The producer then turns the picture over to the music people, usually with the injunction to do a great job cheaply in a couple of weeks. This, on the face of it, is silly, and I have tried to avoid working this way as well as to minimise the delays which are involved to get a picture released because of the time it takes to write, arrange, and record a score. Usually I have had the score in well ahead and I have tried to get these men to do the score from the script, having the weeks and months of production for the job — so that they are in a position to keep up with the changes as we edit the picture and to go

58

with the least possible delay into the scoring, at the same time having had sufficient time during the shooting of the picture to do a good job, instead of being rushed into doing it in a week or so when the picture is finished.

Incredibly, I have met resistance on this, particularly from [composer and conductor] Max Steiner, who found it difficult to do the work in this fashion, claiming that he had to have a finished picture. This was one of my long-standing arguments with Max, and his point in turn was based upon something else which was the root of our decision to get a divorce, which was my objection to what I term 'Mickey Mouse' scoring: an interpretation of each line of dialogue and each movement musically, so that the score tells with music exactly what is being done by the actors on the screen. It has long been my contention that this is ridiculous and that the purpose of a score is to unobtrusively help the mood of each scene without the audience being aware that they are listening to music — and if I am right in this contention, why can't the score be prepared from the script even though cuts and re-arrangements may be necessary after the picture is edited — for the basic selection of music and general arrangement would not be affected by these cuts. I could go into this with you at further length but it would develop into an essay on musical scoring, about which I feel very keenly. I don't think there is another producer in Hollywood that devotes 10 per cent as much time to the score as I do — and it may interest you to know that I was the first producer to use dramatic scores. Max Steiner argued with me at the time, as he has since readily admitted, that musical scoring could not be used without the source of the music being explained to an audience.

I feel now that musical scoring is due for great improvement. Among other things, I feel that we have not had top-notch composers and conductors. I feel too that our pictures have been used as an exploitation ground for the second-rate talents of the composers who have been out here, and who have seen fit to substitute their own compositions for the practically untouched library of the world's music — which in

59

my opinion is a goldmine for emotional effect that requires intelligent and educated selection and arrangement for our purposes by a man who has learned which music plays with most effect upon the emotions of the public. I am not certain that I would argue so much about the use of the world's classical and even non-classical music if I had as an alternative really fine original composition. But too much of what has been composed for my pictures, and everybody else's pictures, has been second rate — and I say this even though I am grateful for what I regard as the excellent composition in some of my pictures, notably Stothart's work in *Viva Villa!* and Steiner's work in *The Garden of Allah.*

Newman has been much more reasonable about working from script than Max was, but he too resisted the use of standard music that I thought could be used effectively and even help in achieving subconsciously a nostalgic mood. On occasion, notably in the score of *Anna Karenina,* I was able to force standard music. In the case of *Karenina,* Tchaikovsky selections — and with good effect.

D.O.S.

'Tchaikovsky selections . . .' Forty-five years on, when we consider the contributions made to original scores by a host of brilliant composers* Selznick's arguments lack credibility. And what about the very real danger of the audience being familiar with the classical masterpieces chosen, with which they associate quite different emotions and events?

Nevertheless, five years later, this particular bee was still firmly in Selznick's bonnet, and this time we are considering the mightiest motion picture of them all.

*Serge Prokofiev, Erich Wolfgang Korngold, Alex North, Ralph Vaughan Williams, Aaron Copland, Jerry Goldsmith, William Walton, Elmer Bernstein, Miklos Rózsa, Dmitri Shostakovich, Georges Auric, Arthur Bliss, Alfred Newman . . . where does one stop? Moreover, I have no doubt that Mozart, Mendelssohn, Mussorgsky and Massenet would have all been willing to attempt film scores, provided the producers of the time hadn't insisted on 'Telemann selections'.

The score of *Intermezzo* is receiving a great deal of comment and extraordinarily favourable attention, for which I thank and congratulate you both.

The outstanding point that has been commented on by so many and that certainly has served to make the score so beautiful, is its use of classical music to such a great extent instead of original music hastily written. This is a point on which I have been fighting for years, with little success. . . .

I have had a dozen people ask me hopefully whether *Gone With the Wind* will give the feeling of the Old South in its whole score — whether the score will be based entirely, or to a large extent, upon the strains and songs and compositions of that particular period and civilisation. And I am increasingly depressed by the prospect that we are not going to use the great classical music of the world for our score, nor are we even going to use the great Southern pieces for a large section of our score. But if we don't, we will have failed to learn the lesson of concert managers, radio broadcasts, and of our own *Intermezzo*.

I should like you both to give this your immediate thought and I should appreciate it if Mr Steiner would adapt whatever his plans are for the score to use, instead of two or three hours of original music, little original music and a score based on the great music of the world, and of the South in particular.

After you have discussed this between yourselves, I should like to see both of you.

D.O.S.
Memo from David O. Selznick
Edited by Rudy Behlmer

The composer of the Gone With the Wind *score, Max Steiner, ignored Selznick's advice and, in so doing, gave us the most famous and memorable romantic theme in cinema history.*

*Lou Forbes was Music Director of Selznick International.

Ten years on, another producer and composer were still involved in the same argument and this last story (again from **Tony Thomas's** *revealing book* Music For The Movies) *goes to show that even composers like* **Aaron Copland** *had no guarantee of the final word in such debates.*

The film for which Aaron Copland won his Oscar is *The Heiress* (1949), which fact has an ironic twist to it. After Copland had recorded the score and returned to New York, the front office at Paramount — and producer-director William Wyler must have been the main voice — decided to remove Copland's title music from the picture and replace it with an arrangement of the song 'Plaisir d'Amour', which was also featured in the course of the storytelling. Copland wrote to the Press disclaiming responsibility for that part of the score. Just how much this damaged the picture is hard to tell; certainly it ruined Copland's intentions of setting the tone and character of the story. His original title has a marked tragic-dramatic mood, suggestive of the complicated life of the young woman who is thwarted by a domineering father and cheated by a shallow lover. The title music for a film is the one spot in the score where a composer can employ strictly musical form and summarise the content of the film. Copland in this instance, like the heiress herself, was thus badly cheated. It was a brutal professional insult yet it was one with a strange rebound — this is the only occasion of a composer winning the coveted gold statuette of the Academy of Motion Picture Arts and Sciences for a score minus its title overture, which is the only part of a score the majority of filmgoers ever consciously hear.

William Wyler and David O. Selznick were both born in 1902. 'Talkies' didn't appear until the mid-1920s, so both men must have spent their formative years with the silent screen. Perhaps they were subconsciously longing for the good old days when it was taken for granted that music for films was chosen from that which already existed. Even as late as 1927 the score for **Cecil B. de Mille's** The King Of Kings *was compiled on this principle, and overleaf is just one of the many 'music sheets' issued for the benefit of the pit orchestras in the cinemas where the film played.*

During 1926, when The King of Kings *was in production, the Australian composer, arranger and pianist* **Percy Grainger** *was also in Hollywood. He got married on the stage of the Hollywood Bowl during a concert of his own music and before a paying audience of 20,000 people.*

Three years later he went to France to visit **Frederick Delius.**

Percy Grainger had been a great favourite of Delius from the day they had met, when Grainger was a fascinating young fellow, full of original ideas, with the energy of a team of men and the looks of an Apollo.

He must have been nearer 50 than 40, but he looked not a day older than 30. He had a fine, arresting, yet rather boyish head, and I liked the look in his eyes. But for his fair bushy hair, one would have thought that here was a professional athlete. He was smaller than I had expected him to be, and moved with all the alacrity of a man very wide awake.

63

Musical Suggestions for
The King of Kings
By ROY ROBERTSON

THEME	Music Suggested
I—Christ	9/4 Section from Hunchback of Notre Dame
II—Mary Magdalen (before conversion)	Karma
III—Blind Girl	6/8 Section of L'Arlesienne Suite No. 4
IV—Mary the Mother	8/8 Section from Hunchback of Notre Dame
V—High Priest	Largo from Dalibor Sel
VI—Caiaphas	Crepuscule D'angoisse
VII—Christ Prayer	Les Perses, from 20
VIII—Miracle Music	Symphonie in E minor (Brass Muted)
IX—Soldiers Mysterious	Cabal
X—Judas	Lohengrin from 4/4

Titles and Action Cues	Music Suggested
Overture	Grand March from Opera Cleopatra
'This is the story'	THEME I
'in Judea'	Persian Suite No. 2
At CU of actor with mirror	Torchlight Dance from Feramors Ballet
'Mary I know'	Allegro Appassionata
As Mary grips actor's neck	Appassionata in A minor from Major Sect.
'Nay, 'twas no woman'	THEME I
As Mary strikes gong	Two cymbal beats (loose)
Segue	THEME II
'Mary I will wager'	Dramatic Dialogue
As chariot arrives	Emotional Agitato
'And it was'	Antar from Allegro, D major
As blind girl appears	THEME III
As blind girl exits	Antar from last 32 bars
As Mark is seen	Ariadne auf Naxos
Spies of the High Priests	THEME VI
As Peter grabs crutch	Sous les Tenailles
As Peter goes to Mark	Les Pheniciennes
As blind girl is seen	THEME III
'And gathered in the House'	D'Albert Suite No. 1
At Mary the Mother spinning	THEME IV
As horn is blown	Trumpet Call (horn if any). Watch screen
Segue	Deluge
At CU of Mary the Mother	THEME IV
As blind girl kneels	L'Arlesienne Suite No. 1 from Poco Lentamente

64

Type of Music	Composer	Publisher
Broad Maestoso	Massenet	Lafleur
Dram. March Maestoso	Herbert	Fischer
Semi-Lullaby	Bizet	Fischer
Sad Flowing	Massenet	Lafleur
Mysterious Flowing	Smetana	Fischer
Mysterious Dramatic	Fosse	Liber
Mysterious Sad	Leroux	Leduc
Mysterious à la Hymn	Pierne	Liber
Mysterious March	Kay	Forster
Dramatic Mysterious	Wagner-Potoker	Fischer

Type of Music	Composer	Publisher
March grand	Mancinelli	Hawkes
Andante 4/4	Rubenstein	Liber
Light 3/4 Moderato	Rubenstein	Fischer
Passionate	Curzon	Dix
Dramatic Agitato	Savino	Francis & Day
Dramatic	Brusselmans	Liber
Dramatic Agitato	Savino	Robins
Dramatic Maestoso	Rimsky-Korsakov	Leduc
Broad Dramatic	Rimsky-Korsakov	Leduc
Light 4/4	Massenet	Leduc
Dramatic Heavy	Fosse	Yves
Maestoso Light	Massenet	Lafleur
Flowing	Becce	Liber
Neutral		
Drama Largo	Urbine	Liber
Sad	Bizet	Fischer

*Where are they now, Becce and Fosse, Urbine and Savino,
Brusselmans?*

The more vigorous sports have never been in my line, but that fortnight I did more chasing about than in all my school-days put together. Up with the blacksmith in the morning, Grainger used to drag me out of bed to go running with him. Now, I should not have minded a gentle trot before breakfast each morning, but when you were expected to gallop along and catch a ring that was being thrown at you like lightning from all angles, to fling it back with equal zest, and to keep up this strenuous performance for as long as you were able, I regretted that I had misspent my sports days idling with a book whilst my more active schoolfellows showed off their prowess before adoring females. This galloping about was not confined to out of doors. Grainger would dash from one room to another, and, bouncing down the staircase in two jumps, fly through the doorway in mid-air and land with a crash beside Delius's carriage halfway across the yard; the old man would shake his head and say that he really could not bear it.

Once when we had gone round to see Brooks, and were sitting on the terrace overlooking his garden, somebody made a remark about an amazing jump he had witnessed; in fact, it was almost as high as the terrace.

'Why, that's nothing,' said Grainger, and, before we could say a word, he had sprung up from his seat, cleared the para-pet, and disappeared from sight!

'Thank God there isn't a greenhouse down there,' said I to Brooks, who was still sitting speechless in his chair. A few seconds later Grainger came running up the steps from the garden, and would have jumped over again had we not forcibly dissuaded him. I had noticed that if he accompanied us on our evening walks, he never left the house with us in the normal way, but always sprang into our midst from a window facing the street. Brooks now began to dare him to do this, and that, and the other, but Grainger could do everything. And when they had said that there was one thing he could not do, namely, to stand on the terrace below the house and from there throw a tennis ball over the house, then run up the dozen steps to the door, through the house, and catch it before it fell into the yard on the other side, and, incredible though it may seem, he had done it three times, I took his arm and led him home, lest in the end he should break his neck.

I had never seen such energy in a man. It was unhuman. He was always impatient when walking, and was for ever wanting to run. He could not understand why we forbade him to gallop up the road with Delius in his carriage! Despite his tremendous energy, he was rarely hungry, ate very little, was a non-smoker, non-drinker, and a vegetarian. Whilst we delighted in the pleasure of the table, he would sit with his bran and his glass of 'Château de Pump' — tepid water with a few drops of milk in it — and Delius would say, 'Jelka, stuff Percy well with oatmeal and macaroni; we know better, don't we, Eric?'

On the first evening on which he played to us, I had walked through the corridor from Delius's bedroom to the music-room to tell Grainger that Delius was ready, when I was astonished to find him patting his knees furiously. Then, when he was black in the face, he sat back, calmed himself and was ready to play. After a very spirited performance of Chopin's B minor Sonata — Delius's favourite work of Chopin — I ventured to ask him about that other performance, to which he replied that it was an exercise which he invariably did before going on to the platform. It consisted of four pats to the second, and this he kept up for a minute and a half. He must always feel excited before he could play.

I tried it for thirty seconds, and could not play at all!

Eric Fenby
Delius as I Knew Him

During this season I made the acquaintance of Percy Grainger. I remember Grieg speaking to me about him; he was very much taken with this promising young pianist. On 17 August Grainger played the Tchaikovsky concerto but I must say I preferred him to play Grieg even though his playing of the Tchaikovsky was energetic and clean-fingered.

Balfour Gardiner gave quite a remarkable concert with my orchestra some years later in which he introduced an entirely British programme, including some of Grainger's now popular works. Grainger collected a number of British folk-tunes, many of which he used as a basis for works like *Molly on the Shore, Shepherd's Hey, Handel in the Strand,* and others. The clog-dance *Handel in the Strand* was originally written for violin, cello and piano, but I scored it for full orchestra as a popular piece for the Promenade concerts. When Grainger heard it he asked me whether Schott's might publish it, a compliment I very much appreciated.

The next-comer of note was Egon Petri, the pupil and friend of Busoni. If his idea was to show England how Liszt should be played he certainly succeeded. After him Donald Francis Tovey (now Sir Donald) in whom Joachim took such lively interest. Tovey's knowledge is encyclopaedic; there seems to be nothing he does not know about old manuscripts.

At this particular concert we had rather an amusing incident with him. In the first half he played a Mozart concerto with his own improvised cadenza. At the rehearsal, of course, we did not stop for the cadenza, but I was rather fearful of it because I never knew whether Tovey's cadenzas were going to last five minutes or fifty. Once he began improvising he lost count of time — in fact, he temporarily left this world altogether. I never met a man with such powers of concentration. When not actually playing during a concerto he would listen intently to the orchestra but with his arms on the top of the piano, elbows out, and tips of his fingers together, his head on his hands. There he would remain, motionless, as though he were saying his prayers. I used to look down at him in apprehension, feeling certain he would never come in on his cue; but sure enough, about four crotchets beforehand, his head would go up and he would be in at the exact moment.

When he was actually playing I think he scared me more still because he *would* place his right foot on the sostenuto pedal and his left behind the stool leg. As his excitement worked up this left leg would stretch out further and further until I was certain the next instant he would fall off the seat and crash his nose on the keys. But he always managed to avoid accidents.

In the second half of this programme he was down to play the Brahms Variations on a Theme of Paganini, Book I. The promenaders crowded round the platform to watch his fingers and gave him a tremendous reception. He came off and asked me whether he should merely return and bow, or play an encore. I thought it might be quicker if he played the encore. 'Yes,' I said. 'Go on and play them a short piece.'

He went on, but I did not think he would sit down and play Book II of the variations — yet that is what he proceeded to do. At ten minutes past eleven I sent the band home and told Percy Pitt to play the national anthem on the organ as soon as Tovey had finished.

Later Tovey gave an orchestral concert with me when I produced his Piano Concerto in A. He was a great writer of programme notes but hardly the kind one can quickly read at a concert. They require study if they are to be appreciated. Hubert Foss eventually persuaded the Oxford University Press to publish then in five volumes under the title: *Essays in Musical Analysis,* and a masterly work it is.

Henry J. Wood
My Life of Music

Essays in Musical Analysis: Beethoven's Symphony No. 5 in C minor, Opus 67.

This work shares with Beethoven's Seventh Symphony the distinction of being not only among the most popular but also among the least misunderstood of musical classics. It has not failed to inspire 'roaring cataracts of nonsense' from

69

commentators, but the nonsense has, for the most part, been confined to technical matters of little concern to the naïve (or ideal) listener; though one heresy I shall discuss here, since on it depends one's whole view of the difference between real composition and mere manufacture. Another immensely lucky fact conducive to the popular appreciation of this symphony is that the famous phrase (made still more famous by Robert Louis Stevenson in *The Ebb Tide*) — the phrase which describes the theme of the first movement as 'destiny knocking at the door' — is no mere figment of a commentator, but is Beethoven's very own words. Mistakes and misreadings in this mighty work have been as frequent as anywhere; the very band-parts issued under the auspices of the 'critical' edition have some scandalously stupid editorial alterations; but not even the notorious old trick of changing the first three quavers into crotchets has been able to make any headway against the overwhelming power and clearness of the whole.

Some good, however, may be done by denouncing the heresy which preaches that 'the whole first movement is built up of the initial figure of four notes'. It is well worth refuting, for it has led to most of the worst features of that kind of academic music which goes furthest to justify the use of the words 'academic' as a term of vulgar abuse. No great music has ever been built from an initial figure of four notes. As I have said elsewhere, you might as well say that every piece of music is built from an initial figure of *one* note. You may profitably say that the highest living creatures have begun from the single nucleated cell. But no ultra-microscope has yet unravelled the complexities of the single living cell; nor, if the spectroscope is to be believed, are we yet very fully informed of the complexities of a single atom of iron: and it is quite absurd to suppose that the evolution of a piece of music can proceed from 'a simple figure of four notes' on lines in the least resembling those of nature. As far as I know, Weingartner is the first writer who has pointed out the truth that the first movement of the C minor

70

Symphony is really remarkable for the length of its sentences; that the first sentences, instead of being 'built up' from a single figure, *break up* into other sentences of even greater variety and breadth; and that the composer who first really 'built up' symphonic movements out of short figures was not Beethoven but Schumann, whose handling of the larger forms became sectional, diffuse, and yet stiff for this very reason.

Obviously the same argument applies to the whole theory of Wagnerian *Leitmotif*. Wagner attained full mastery over the broadest sweep of sequence that music has yet achieved. This alone suffices to refute the orthodox Wagnerian belief that his music is 'built up' from the scraps of theme to which it can be reduced by its dramatic associations, and by the general possibility of articulating big phrases into small figures.

In the first fine careless rapture of Wagnerian analysis it was discovered that the 'four taps', with which 'destiny knocks at the door' in the first movement, recur elsewhere; once (quite accidentally, though in an impressive passage) in the slow movement, and very prominently in the second theme of that dream of terror which we technically call the scherzo.... This profound discovery was supposed to reveal an unsuspected unity in the work; but it does not seem to have been carried far enough. It conclusively proves that the Sonata Appassionata, the G major Pianoforte Concerto, the third movement of the Quartet, Opus 74, and, with the final consummation of a fifth tap, the Violin Concerto, all belong to the C minor Symphony; for the same rhythmic figure pervades them too. The simple truth is that Beethoven could not do without just such purely rhythmic figures at this stage of his art. It was absolutely necessary that every inner part in his texture should assert its own life; but at the same time it was equally necessary that it should not cause constant or rapid changes of harmony by doing so. Figures that can identify a theme while remaining on one note are the natural response to these requirements.

Donald Francis Tovey

71

Writing about music itself is one of the most difficult tasks in the trade, but it has to be done and, like everything else it can be done well or badly. Readers may place the three examples which follow in their own order of merit but, for me, the last (by the American pianist **Charles Rosen***) is the finest description of a single piece of music I have ever read.*

First, though, a trenchant comment on the subject from **Neville Cardus** *and, indirectly, George Bernard Shaw.*

It has always been a mystery to me why music critics make a parade of technical language; contrary motion, chromaticism, modulation, and so on. A musician already knows whether a chord is a dominant ninth or a diminished seventh; the average layman doesn't know what it means. If a critic says that the structure of a work is complex, the texture diaphanous, and the key-sequences progressive, it will not mean anything to most readers; as for the musician, he will know it already or he can find it out for himself. So the critic has fallen between two stools.

You don't find a drama critic talking about the inverted stresses in *Macbeth*; we don't contemplate Virgil only in terms of spondees and dactyls. Shaw in the 1890s wrote a marvellous parody of the scientific style of music criticism. He showed how a drama critic — if he were to write in the same way that dry-as-a-bone music critics do, with all their supertonics — would disembowel Hamlet's 'To be, or not to be':

> Shakespeare, dispensing with the customary exordium, announces the subject at once in the infinitive, after a short connecting passage in which, brief as it is, we recognise the alternative and negative forms on which so much of the significance of the repetition depends. Here we reach a colon; and a pointed pository phrase, in

which the accent falls decisively on the relative pronoun, brings us to the first full-stop.

Conversations with Cardus

If a concentrated week of Webern at the Barbican was not enough to assuage the ardent enthusiast, there was yet another performance, the third in five days, of his Symphony Opus 21 in the Lontano Ensemble's Purcell Room concert last night.

With that musically sharp but unobtrusive perspicacity that invariably characterises her conducting, Odaline de la Martinez directed her players in an account of the symphony's highly condensed music that was not only equally candid and astute but which held an attentive balance between formal and structural clarity, cogent lyrical impulse and, in the second movement variations, tautly aphoristic drama.

Robert Henderson
Daily Telegraph, 16 December 1983

The still unpublished Third Symphony of Brahms is a feast for the critic, who must subsequently describe how it looks and what its beauties are. It is neither one of the rarest nor one of the most inexplicable of misfortunes that the eloquence of the critics declines in inverse proportion to that of the composer. The language of prose is not only poorer than that of music; as far as music is concerned, it is no language at all, since music cannot be translated into it. This may not have meant so much in former and less demanding times. But if one reads today the best of the reviews which appeared immediately following the first performances of the Beethoven Symphonies, and imagines himself in the place of the first reader, one must confess that, while he has sensed the proclamation of great and beautiful music, he has been vouchsafed hardly a hint of its individual physiognomy. Only after the Beethoven symphonies had become generally known, and when critics were able to refer to what the reader himself had already heard and experienced, did we gain the substantial instruction of the better Beethoven studies of our own time. The new Brahms symphony has yet to build such a bridge between critic and reader. The former is left with no other recourse than to compare it with earlier and better-known works of the same master.

Hans Richter, in a gracious toast, recently christened the new symphony 'Eroica'. Actually, if one were to call Brahms's First Symphony the 'Appassionata' and the second the 'Pastoral', then the new symphony might well be called the 'Eroica'. The title is, to be sure, not fully applicable, since only the first and last movements strike us as 'heroic'. In his Symphony in C minor, Brahms plunged with desperate passion into a dark Faustian struggle in the very first dissonant measures. The Finale, with its reminiscences of the last movements of Beethoven's Ninth, does not, for all its ultimate achievements, change the essentially emotional, almost pathological character of the composition. It is the expression of a suffering, abnormally agitated individual. The Symphony No. 2 is a peaceful, often pastoral counterpart. While the thunder of the old Beethoven is still heard receding in the distance, we hear the voices of Mozart and Haydn as if from celestial sanctuary. The Symphony No. 3 is really something new. It repeats neither the unhappy fatalism of the first, nor the cheerful idyll of the second; its foundation is self-confident, rough-and-ready strength. The 'heroic' element in it has nothing to do with anything military, nor does it lead to any tragic dénouement, such as the Funeral March of Beethoven's 'Eroica'. Its musical characteristics recall the healthy soundness of Beethoven's second period, never the eccentricities of his last. And here and there are suggestions of the romantic twilight of Schumann and Mendelssohn.

The first movement belongs among the most signficant and

74

masterly compositions Brahms has given us. Wonderful is the way in which, after two resounding chords in the winds, the belligerent theme of the violins plunges down from above and then soars proudly upwards again. The whole movement gives the impression of having been created in the flush of an inspired hour. Its second theme, in A flat, blends incomparably with the movement as a whole. The climax in the development section is of impressive dimensions but, surprisingly, gives way towards the end to a gradually calmer mood, which, in turn, fades away swiftly and beautifully. The two middle movements prepare the listener for no mighty convulsions; they are rather an invitation to peaceful repose. The slow movement does not sing of deathly depression, nor the fast movement of heavenly exhilaration. They are moderate in pace and expression, tender and gracious in sentiment. The slow movement is a very simple song dialogue between the winds and the deeper strings. It would not be out of place in a Brahms serenade. Short, and without organic development or climax, it provides surprises and effects of tone colour suggesting the musical conversation of softly sounding, tuned bells. The Scherzo is represented by an Allegretto in C minor, superficially reminiscent of Mendelssohn, which hovers easily in that hybrid, indeterminate mood which Brahms so favours in his middle movements. The piece is simply scored (without trumpets, trombones, and kettledrums) and is rendered particularly effective by the spirited charm of a middle section in A flat.

For all their fundamental differences, Brahms's First and Third Symphonies are similar in one important respect: their respective middle movements are rather too small scaled, in content as well as in extent, for the imposing movements which adjoin them. The Finale of the Symphony No. 3 is again an accomplishment of the first order, the equal of the first movement, if not its superior. It rolls upon us with a fast, sultry figure in the deep strings. The theme as such is not impressive, but it immediately experiences the most astonishing development. The eerie sultriness of the opening is discharged in a magnificent storm, exalting and refreshing. The intensity of the music increases continuously. The second theme in C major, brilliantly and emphatically intoned by the horn, soon makes way for a third, in C minor, even more forcefully introduced. At the peak of all this imposing development, one naturally expects a brilliant, triumphal conclusion. But with Brahms, and with Brahms alone, it is well to be prepared for the unexpected. This Finale moves imperceptibly from the key of F minor to that of D major, the raging winds subside to a mysterious whisper — long sustained chords in the winds are interrupted by the light rustlings of the muted violins and violas in thirds and sixths. The movement draws to a close, strangely, inconclusively, but most beautifully.

Many music lovers may prefer the titanic force of the First, others the untroubled charm of the Second. But the Third strikes me as artistically the most perfect. It is more compactly made, more transparent in detail, more plastic in the main themes. The orchestration is richer in novel and charming combinations. In ingenious modulations it is equal to the best of Brahms's works; and in the free association of contrary rhythms, of which Brahms is so fond and in the handling of which he is such a master, it has the virtue of not seeking effects at the cost of intelligibility.

Eduard Hanslick
Music Criticisms

Gaspard de la Nuit, Trois poèmes d'après Aloysius Bertrand, is Ravel's homage to the nineteenth century. It might be called the *Tombeau de Liszt.* These three pieces are the most extravagantly imaginative works of tone-painting for the keyboard, and the last great contributions to nineteenth century virtuoso piano technique. And as for precision of imagination in keyboard writing, no one has ever surpassed the last page of *Ondine,* with its great splash and the concentric circles that grow wider and wider as the water returns to its former calm.

The splash is, indeed, an invention of Ravel's and is not to be found in the poem from *Gaspard de la Nuit* on which the music is based. The book itself still has imaginative force; Baudelaire admired (and was influenced by) the author, Jacques Louis Napoléon Bertrand born in 1807, who later took the Christian name of Aloysius, which sounds more romantic to French ears than to English or American ones. His one book, a series of short prose poems never published during his lifetime, is everything that we like to consider late romanticism — perverse, diabolic, and sentimental. The three poems chosen by Ravel give him admirable possibilities for tone-painting: water, a tolling bell, and a gnome — music based on poems which are themselves, as the author said, 'engravings after imaginary pictures'.

Ondine, however, differs from most musical representations of water in that it seems not only to picture the water itself and catch its sound, but to portray the vibration of lights reflected from it. The basis of the music is not the plaintive melody that represents the song of the nymph, but the irregular, syncopated tremolo which opens the piece, and which is transformed into so many different versions and played in all the registers of the piano. It pervades the music so completely that, at the end, an arpeggio which merely repeats the harmony is enough to give the impression that one is hearing the shimmering vibration of the opening bars once again. Continuously surrounded by this vibration and held together by it, the endless melody seems hardly to move as it progresses to its enormous climax two-thirds of the way through the piece.

Another syncopated irregular ostinato rhythm, this time a very slow one, is the basis of the second piece, *Le Gibet.* A B flat in the middle register of the piano represents the tolling of the bell in the distance as the hanged man silently swings to and fro on the gallows. The bell tolls ceaselessly from one

77

end of the piece to the other, an endless organ point, which is finally left suspended as if to continue in the listener's imagination until broken off by the beginning of the next piece. The music is an assault on the nerves of the listener, a creation of tension through insistence, like the Chinese water torture. Even the sonority is deliberately limited: the soft pedal is to be held down throughout, although this does not prevent Ravel from creating a variety of nuances. What is most amazing is the breadth, the spaciousness of the sonority emphasised by the massive thickness of the harmony and the steady rhythm. The interest of the piece lies in the firm, tense line of the melody, the conflict of accents between it and the steady beat and irregular rhythm of the bell, and the subtle contrasts of sonority — contrasts which seem (like *Ondine*) to portray changes of light, as when the atmosphere grows darker and blurs in the wonderful series of chords moving softly in contrary motion over almost the whole range of the keyboard. *Scarbo* — gnome, imp, dwarf or bogey of Bertrand's prose poem — becomes a demon in the third and last piece of Ravel. In this work the whole virtuoso tradition finds at last its *raison d'être* — the portrayal of sheer terror. The main pleasure of hearing (or rather, watching) a virtuoso performance is really close to the pleasure of watching a tightrope walker, or any acrobat — the clutch of fear that he will fall, that something will go wrong, that he can't keep it up. Virtuosos are, indeed, classed as acrobats and feel unnaturally aggrieved. Music which not only is, but *sounds,* difficult is essential to the emotional atmosphere of *Scarbo. Scarbo* is, in one sense, the most abstract of the three parts of *Gaspard de la Nuit;* only the sudden blowing up of the imp into a giant, and, at the end, his disappearance into the air are graphically and precisely rendered, in contrast to the specific programme and visual references of *Ondine* and *Le Gibet.* In another sense, however, *Scarbo* is the least abstract; it is the most direct attack on the nerves and the emotions of the listener.

The form and structure of *Scarbo* are unique. It is the only successful application for the piano, that I can call to mind, of the methods of Strauss's tone poems. The form, which is not complicated, is not, however, easily reducible to a simple formula in words: it could be awkwardly described as the welding together of a number of short motives into a rhythmic structure that builds up in a series of waves. There are three short motives in *Scarbo:* a leap, a repeated note (which later takes two forms — one of them a guitar-like, strumming figure) and a twitch. These are continually combined like tiny stones in a mosaic, and unified in a magnificently tense rhythm, which alternately sounds like a terribly fast waltz and a Spanish serenade. The music has at times a sinister gaiety, but always the irrational terror of a nightmare. Behind all the brilliant surface play of *Gaspard de la Nuit,* even behind the terror of *Le Gibet* and *Scarbo,* is an overpowering nostalgia, a hopeless desire for a past that never existed that Ravel himself creates. It pervades the whole of his music wherever we look — the *Mother Goose Suite* with its fairy-tale background and its continuous melancholy; *La Valse,* almost necrophilic in the way that it turns the Viennese atmosphere into a ghostly one, deader and more desirable than ever.

Charles Rosen
Columbia record sleeve, 1960

Another aspect of writing about music concerns not what it is, how to listen to it, or what impression it makes, but how to perform it.

79

For most professionals the score itself is usually enough, because musical notation is a vocabulary of enormous variety and flexibility, but once in a while a piece, or a performance, so captures people's imagination that there is an instant demand to know 'how it's done'. Such a piece, and such a performance, took millions by storm for over thirty years, Rachmaninoff's playing of his own Prelude in C sharp minor.

This advice, from the horse's mouth, is a model of simple clarity and precise thought.

Absolute music (to which this prelude belongs) can suggest or induce a mood in the listener; but its primal function is to give intellectual pleasure by the beauty and variety of its form. This was the end sought by Bach in his wonderful series of preludes, which are a source of unending delight to the educated musical listener. Their salient beauty will be missed if we try to discover in them the mood of the composer. If we must have the psychology of the prelude, let it be understood that its function is not to express a mood, but to induce it.

The prelude, as I conceive it, is a form of absolute music, intended, as its name signifies, to be played before a more important piece of music or as an introduction to some function. The form has grown to be used for music of an independent value. But so long as the name is given to a piece of music, the work should in some measure carry out the significance of the title.

For example, in the work under consideration, I endeavour to arrest attention by the opening theme. These three notes, proclaimed in unison in treble and bass, should boom solemnly and portentously. After this introduction the three-note melody runs through the first section of twelve bars, and counter to it, in both clefs, runs a contrasted melody in chords. Here we have two distinct melodic movements working against each other, and the effect is to arrest the attention of the listener.

The nature of the principal theme is that of a massive foundation against which the melody in the chords furnishes a contrast to lighten up the gloom. If worked out too long the effect would be one of monotony, so a middle movement intervenes quickly. The change of mood is abrupt, and for twenty-nine bars the music sweeps along like a rising storm, gaining in intensity as the melody mounts upward. The movement is carried out in single notes instead of chords, and at the climax the original movement re-enters with everything doubled both in right and left hands. After this outburst has spent itself, the music grows gradually more quiet and a coda of seven bars brings the work to a close.

The listener has been aroused, stimulated, and then quieted. His mind is alert and open for what follows. The prelude has filled its office.

If the pupil must have his mental status fixed, let him keep in mind what I have just said. Then let him study carefully the anatomy of the composition. The divisions of the work are simple.

The first technical caution is to strike just the right pace in the proclamation of the opening theme and then maintain that pace strictly throughout the first section. One common mistake is to play this opening theme too loudly. I admit there is great temptation to pound it; but the climax does not come at the outset. I have marked these three notes *ff.* You will find several *fff* marks later on. So save your strength. The chords of the intervening melody should be pressed out lightly and caressingly, and the player should be careful to make the top note in the right-hand chords sing. The mistakes to avoid are the tendency to strike these chords unevenly or with an arpeggio effect and to lose the evenness of pace. The difficulty in the first section will be to maintain this evenness through the third and fourth beat in each bar.

The three notes of the first theme are not to be struck too loudly but with sufficient force to make the tones carry through.

In the agitated section the melody in the right is carried by the first note in each group. But for this I might have marked the passage 'allegro con fuoco'. The player must accommodate his pace to his technical ability. He must not hurry the passage beyond his capacity to make the melody stand out.

The repetition of the first movement in doubled octaves calls for all the force the player is capable of. The pupil must be cautioned against mistaking fury for breadth and majesty. It will be safer to take this passage even a trifle more slowly than at the opening, and above all have regard for the evenness of the decrescendo. I begin to let this effect become apparent after the sixth bar of this movement.

Notice particularly that the melody in the coda is carried by the middle notes of the chords in both the right and left hands. These notes must be accentuated slightly. Beware of the temptation to arpeggiate the final chords.

Sergei Rachmaninoff
'My Prelude in C sharp minor', February 1910

Rachmaninoff's prelude reached the height of its popularity when home-grown music was much more fashionable than it is today. When thousands of sitting-rooms boasted a piano, and hundreds of uncles boasted a voice; when one made music for oneself and one's friends.

Writing in 1934 **Edwin Evans** *uses the pastime as the basis for a definition:*

The most admirable recent definition of the term 'chamber music' is that which describes it as the music of friends. Though much of it is now performed in public, it is essentially the music of those who come together to make music for themselves, as distinct from those who gather at concerts to have music made for them. Soloists rarely play or sing to themselves, except for study or practice, and even an amateur orchestra comes together with the view of eventually performing to an audience, but the true devotees of chamber music have no need of an audience for the enjoyment of their pursuit. They find it in the interplay of individualities, in the dovetailing of their individual contributions to the whole. They meet as friends and admit a few friends to their intimacy. That is the real spirit of chamber music, by this it was animated during a great part of its history, and this still inspires countless private societies in which it is cultivated for the sheer joy of performing it.

Edwin Evans
The Musical Companion
Edited by A.L. Bacharach

I think it may be valid to extend that definition to cover jazz as well. The more I think about it, the more it seems to me that most of the best jazz is also the music of friends.

Many descriptions by Duke's musicians exist of typical recording sessions, which would usually start with Duke arriving late and sitting at the piano doodling for fifteen minutes as he warmed up. If the tempo was fast, the band knew the first number would be swinging; if slow, they were prepared for a lament. Once Duke's humming and strumming was over, he'd suggest they see if the piano was in tune, which meant that the band should tune up. They'd already done so, but Ellington wanted to hear the tones before he'd go any further. This, in the words of Rex Stewart, is what happened next:

> Then the fun begins as Duke reaches into his pocket, and with the air of a magician produces some scraggy pieces of manuscript paper — about one-eighth of a page on which he's scribbled some notes. I recall one occasion when he'd jotted some notes for the saxophones, but there was nothing for Johnny Hodges. Duke had the

saxes run the sequence down twice, while Johnny sat nonchalantly smoking. Then Duke called to Hodges, 'Hey, Rabbit, give me a long slow glissando against that progression. Yeah! That's it!' Next he said to Cootie Williams, 'Hey, Coots, you come in on the second bar, in a subtle manner, growling softly like a hungry little lion cub that wants his dinner but can't find his mother. Try that, OK?' Following that, he'd say, 'Deacon,' (how Lawrence Brown hated that nickname) 'you are cast in the role of the sun beating down on the scene. What kind of a sound do you feel that could be? You don't know? Well, try a high B flat in a felt hat, play it legato, and sustain it for eight bars. Come on, let's all hit this together,' and that's the way things went — sometimes.

Derek Jewell
'Duke' — a portrait of Duke Ellington

When jazz moves on to the concert platform, however, the complications begin.

In those days Paul Whiteman was still 'the King of Jazz', with no rivals in sight. Starting out from Santa Barbara in California, he had conquered successively Los Angeles, Atlantic City and New York. He had a million-dollar income. He controlled eleven bands in New York, seventeen on the road, and received royalties from forty more bands which played his arrangements. In New York he was established in the Palais nightclub, but he was visibly present in other places — he played on special occasions at hotels, at marriages, at weddings, for George White's *Scandals* and for phonograph companies. In the spring of 1923 he made a triumphal progress through Europe and returned to America more famous then ever.

It was Paul Whiteman's belief that jazz deserved to be

elevated to the stature of great music. 'Jazz,' he declared, 'is the music of our time, and we are not living in an age of decadence. Jazz is the voice of our age.' He was not the first to make such claims, but he was the first who could afford to assemble a complete orchestra in a public hall, train his musicians and provide a complete programme of jazz for the delectation of music lovers. Towards the end of 1923 he was already planning his programme. He discussed it with Gershwin and received the half promise of a composition of some length on a jazz theme.

Gershwin was so busy with *Sweet Little Devil* that he paid little attention to Whiteman's plans until one day early in January 1924 when he read an announcement in the *New York Tribune,* saying that he was at work on a jazz concerto for Whiteman. The report added that Irving Berlin was writing a syncopated tone poem and Victor Herbert was busy composing an American suite. The programme, designed to answer the question, 'What is American music?' was scheduled to take place at Aeolian Hall during the afternoon of 12 February in the presence of Sergei Rachmaninov, Jascha Heifetz, and Efrem Zimbalist. Gershwin had little more than a month in which to compose the concerto, have it orchestrated and rehearsed.

Gershwin called Whiteman on the telephone. What puzzled him more than anything else was the date — 12 February. Whiteman explained that someone else was thinking of putting on a similar programme later in the same month. It was necessary to advance the programme at Aeolian Hall.

'Will you do it, George?' Whiteman asked.

'Yes, but I'll need Ferde Grofe to orchestrate it,' Gershwin replied. 'I won't have time to do the orchestration, even if I was sure I could orchestrate it properly. I'll write it as a piano concerto.'

'That's how I want it,' Whiteman said. 'Let me know as soon as you are ready.'

Gershwin worked best under pressure. He possessed supreme self-assurance. He went to work at once, assembling and discarding ideas for a 'blues' concerto, but for some reason none of the thematic material he had accumulated pleased him. He was in love with Liszt's Second Hungarian Rhapsody, and the rhapsodic form appealed to him. Gradually there emerged a general theme, very shapeless and diffuse, rhapsodic in nature, beginning nowhere and ending nowhere. He was on the train journeying to Boston for the première of *Sweet Little Devil* when the concerto for the first time came into focus. The train whistles, the rattle of the wheels, the strange symphonic sounds which even the unmusical can hear in the confused roar of a train as it moves rapidly — all these things excited him, until by the time he reached Boston, the complete construction of the rhapsody was present in his mind. The *Rhapsody in Blue* is many things, but it includes the description of a train journey as its central element.

The train journey supplied the beginning and the end. The middle section came into focus a week later when he returned to New York and found himself improvising at a party. 'When I am in my normal mood,' he said once, 'music drips from my fingers.' He was in a normal mood at the party. One theme after another dripped from his fingers, but suddenly a 'blues' theme, one that had long haunted him, took possession of him, and he began to play it with the air of someone who has at last found what he was looking for. This brief and melancholy theme fitted exactly into the middle section of the rhapsody. The *Rhapsody in Blue* was now virtually completed.

In three weeks he completed the rhapsody, with Ferde Grofe at his elbow, preparing the orchestration while the ink was still wet on the page. Gershwin revised till the last minute; so did Grofe. There were four or five complete rehearsals at the Palais Royal with Gershwin playing the piano, and a number of changes were introduced into the rehearsals, the most important being the insertion of a rising passage ending in a fermata, suggested by Victor Herbert. Not all the score was written down. Since the piano solo part was to be played by Gershwin at the concert, and he knew exactly at what point he could improvise, he simply left a gap on the manuscript and told Whiteman 'to wait for a nod' where the orchestra was to come in. It was a palpably dangerous arrangement, but it had the virtue of adding freshness to the material.

On the morning of the concert Whiteman suffered from a failure of nerve. He was very frightened. He had spent a large amount of his own money, hired nine additional musicians, and he was beginning to wonder whether there were advantages in abandoning the concert. He had invited the most famous musicians of the time to attend. Rachmaninoff, Godowsky, Stokowski, Walter Damrosch, Jascha Heifetz, Mischa Elman, John Philip Sousa, John McCormack and Igor Stravinsky had all been invited, and all had accepted the invitation. By midday he was a little calmer, but in the early afternoon, when snow began falling, he was more worried than ever. He went to the entrance of Aeolian Hall, saw a huge mob of people clamouring to get in, and thought he had come to the wrong place, until he saw Victor Herbert struggling in the crowd. He learned the next day that the house could have been sold ten times over.

He was more depressed than ever when he went backstage. He vowed he would give $5,000 if he could stop the performance, which had already cost him $7,000. He was not particularly impressed by the programme he was offering, and even had some doubts about the *Rhapsody in Blue.* It was a very strange programme beginning with 'Livery Stable Blues' and ending with Sir Edward Elgar's *Pomp and Circumstance.* Of the twenty-six numbers, Gershwin's was the twenty-fifth. Included among the numbers was a semi-symphonic arrangement of Irving Berlin's 'Orange Blossoms in California', and a suite of serenades in Spanish, Chinese, and Cuban styles. Twenty-three musicians formed the ensemble. It was a very long programme, and an exceedingly pretentious one.

The most boring part of the programme was the long introductory address by Hugh Ernst which described the

87

educational nature of the programme and the singular validity of Paul Whiteman's orchestra, which was encouraging and bringing to birth a new form of American music. It was not unlike those addresses which are heard periodically in high school auditoriums, and the audience began to be restless. It was more restless than ever by the time the entr'acte came along. The hall was overheated, and the standees were beginning to make their way out. Fatigue, inertia, the most exquisite configurations of boredom had set in when at long last Paul Whiteman, himself bored and confused and close to tears, announced the first public performance of the *Rhapsody in Blue*.

Gershwin stepped out from the wings and took his place at the piano. He shot a single glance at the conductor, and then the baton was raised sharply to introduce the long clarinet wail, like the sound of a steam whistle as a train emerges from a tunnel or like the sound of an explosion in the brain, which introduces the rhapsody. Ross Gorman was Whiteman's clarinettist, and he played those seventeen broken notes brilliantly, bringing the audience immediately to attention. The audience craned forward. Something new and startling was being performed, all the more desirable because it had come after a long period of waiting. Halfway through Paul Whiteman lost his place and surrendered to a sudden inexplicable fit of weeping. He recovered himself some eleven pages later, and afterwards he wondered how the orchestra had performed during the interval. At the end there was an ovation. Gershwin hurried off the stage to bandage his fingers. He had pounded so hard that there was blood on the keys.

Robert Payne
Gershwin

The most profound truths, the most blasphemous things, the most terrible ideas, may be incorporated within the walls of a symphony, and the police none the wiser. It is its freedom from the meddlesome hand of the censor that makes of music a playground for great brave souls.

James Huneker
Mezzotints in Modern Music

The première of the Thirteenth Symphony was awaited in Moscow with intense anticipation. The excitement generated was not purely musical: people were aware of the artistic tensions behind the scene, of the meetings between the arts intelligentsia and the Party. The city was buzzing with rumours of a possible last-minute cancellation of the performance. The dress rehearsal was open to Conservatory students and faculty members. A staff member of the Glinka Museum emerged from the dress rehearsal; my question about the music was waved aside, '. . . but the *words*'.

At the première, the government box remained unoccupied, and a planned television transmission did not take place. A listener approaching the Conservatory Hall on the evening of 18 December found the entire square cordoned off by police. Inside, the hall was filled to overflowing. The first half, consisting of Mozart's 'Jupiter' Symphony, received a minimum of attention; no one cared . . . . The intermission seemed endless; finally, the chorus filed on stage, followed by the orchestra, the soloist, the conductor Kyril Kondrashin. The tension was unbearable. The first movement, *Babyi Yar,* was greeted with a burst of spontaneous applause. At the end of the hour-long work, there was an ovation rarely witnessed. On the stage was Shostakovich, shy and awkward, bowing stiffly. He was joined by Yevtushenko, moving with the ease of a born actor. Two great artists — a generation apart — fighting for the same cause — freedom of the human spirit.

Seeing the pair together, the audience went wild; the rhythmic clapping, so characteristic of Russian enthusiasm, redoubled in intensity, the cadenced shouts 'Bra-vo Shos-ta-ko-vich' and 'Bra-vo Yev-tu-shen-ko' filled the air. The audience seemed to be carried away as much by the music as by the words, although (contrary to custom) the texts were not printed in the programme distributed to the public.

The following morning, a one-sentence report appeared in *Pravda*, an absurd anti-climax for anyone who had witnessed the exciting evening. I rushed to the headquarters of the Composers' Union in search of a score or a piano reduction; I wanted to reread the texts and evaluate their relationship to the music. My request was met with polite head-shaking and evasive excuses — the 'only' available score was in the hands of a critic who had failed to return it . . . . Needless to say it was never 'returned', and all my efforts to have a glimpse of the score remained fruitless. Only later did I realise that this was no accident: there was an 'embargo' on the score because of official dissatisfaction with certain sections of the work.

Boris Schwarz
Music and Musical Life in Soviet Russia 1917—1970

There's two kinds of music, good and bad. If you like it, it's good — if you don't, it's bad.

Harry James
Quoted in a television broadcast, July 1983

If nobody wants to go to your concert, nothing will stop them.

Isaac Stern

As we conversed on modern music, Stanford Robinson said he thought it was sad that so few works gave pleasure to both audience and performers. 'The tragedy of it is that few of my contemporaries write symphonic music that can be enjoyed at its first hearing by the majority of musical people,' he complained. 'Even many of those who *do* listen to it seem to do so only out of a sense of duty: they feel they *ought* to give it a hearing, even if they gain little pleasure from it. But this problem is not merely one of the audience. Many an enterprising conductor can remember occasions when his orchestra has made it perfectly obvious to him at rehearsal that it neither likes nor understands the music over which he, through previous study, is enthusiastic. Of course, if the conductor himself is bored with it . . .'

Robinson told me that he had been present at first performances of many modern works and had talked with the performers afterwards. 'If that's modern music, I don't like it', 'Awful stuff', 'Couldn't make head nor tail of it' and 'Let's hope it'll be the first and last performance', were typical of the remarks he had heard, particularly when the work had not been adequately rehearsed, for it is often only after much study that a conductor and his orchestra begin to enjoy a modern work. 'How then can a layman enjoy it at first or second hearing?' Robinson asks, '. . . and if he doesn't, how can he be persuaded to come and listen to it again and again until he does? There is the problem of modern music.'

Donald Brook
Conductor's Gallery

We look for new sonorities, new intervals, new forms. Where it will lead, I don't know. I don't want to know. It would be like knowing the date of my death.

Pierre Boulez

Arnold Schoenberg, *on being told his violin concerto demanded a six-fingered soloist:*

'I can wait.'

I occasionally play works by contemporary composers and for two reasons. First, to discourage the composer from writing any more, and secondly to remind myself how much I appreciate Beethoven.

Jascha Heifetz
Life, 28 July 1961

A young composer came to Brahms and asked if he might play for the master a funeral march he had composed in memory of Beethoven. Well, permission was granted, and the young man earnestly played away. When he was through, he sought Brahms's opinion. 'I tell you,' said the great man candidly, 'I'd be much happier if you were dead and Beethoven had written the march.'

André Previn
Music Face to Face, 1971

I like to look on the composer's vocation as the old troubadours or bards did. In those days it was no disgrace for a man to be turned on to step in front of an army and inspire them with a song. I know that there are a lot of people who like to celebrate events with music: to these people I have given tunes. Is that wrong? Why should I write a fugue or something that won't appeal to anyone, when the people yearn for things which can stir them?

Sir Edward Elgar

The Best Time to Compose an Overture

Wait until the evening before opening night. Nothing primes inspiration more than necessity, whether it be the presence of a copyist waiting for your work or the prodding of an impresario tearing his hair. In my time, all the impresarios in Italy were bald at 30.

I composed the overture to *Otello* in a little room in the Barbaja Palace wherein the baldest and fiercest of directors had forcibly locked me with a lone plate of spaghetti and the threat that I would not be allowed to leave the room alive until I had written the last note.

I wrote the overture to *La Gazza Ladra* the day of its opening in the theatre itself, where I was imprisoned by the director and under the surveillance of four stagehands who were instructed to throw my original text through the window, page by page, to the copyists waiting below to transcribe it. In default of pages, they were ordered to throw me out the window bodily.

I did better with *The Barber.* I did not compose an overture, but selected for it one which was meant for a semi-serious opera called *Elisabetta.* The public was completely satisfied.

I composed the overture to *Conte Ory* while fishing, with my feet in the water, and in company of Signor Agnado who

93

talked of Spanish finance. The overture for *William Tell* was composed under more or less similar circumstances. And as for *Mosè,* I did not write one.

Gioacchino Rossini
Letter to an unknown composer

One other phase of music now presents itself, a brief consideration of which must close this chapter. It is the development of opera after Mozart. The operas of Mozart have a realistic, sober psychological truth that is as profound as it is brilliant and incomparable. But early in the nineteenth century a movement began that has been called the romantic movement, but which would be better described as the self-conscious movement. For the first time, perhaps, musicians began to compose with one eye on their audience (even if it was only an audience of one, the composer himself) to watch the success of their effects. With this was born a new type of 'artist' described vividly in modern jargon as a 'stunt-merchant'. The greatest of the 'stunt merchants' were respectively a German, a Jew, and a Frenchman — Wagner (1813—83), Meyerbeer (1791—1864) and Berlioz (1803—69). Two of them, Wagner and Berlioz, were men of astonishing musical genius, and Meyerbeer was a musician of great talent. Between them they set the world talking about themselves as no musician had ever thought of doing before. It is significant that both Wagner and Berlioz were brilliant journalists and propagandists; but

94

it was Wagner especially who set himself the task of advertising himself and his music by means of his writings on a grand scale. It must be admitted that Berlioz was a true innovator and creator, and that his style is purer than Wagner's, both in music and prose. Personally I incline to believe that Wagner was the most self-deceiving musician of genius who has ever lived, but that he had no choice in the matter, since in order to do justice to his genius he had to develop a corresponding fiction.

It is commonly thought that Wagner wrote the poems or librettos of his music dramas first, and his music afterwards. It is no doubt true to this extent, that he actually wrote down and published the words before the notes; but the words are such pure nonsense — by which I mean they are mere words borrowed from many sources, having no real individual content — that they could only have been written down by Wagner with the music already in his mind. The musical associations already in his mind gave them an emotional content. Otherwise, even he would have noticed that they were, in themselves, empty of meaning. In short, Wagner set *words* to his *music* as arbitrarily as any of the Italian composers whom he despises had set their music to words. A true relation between words and music in Wagner's operas does not exist, because the words and the plot have no real independent meaning.

In proof of this I need only state the fact that the essential parts of all Wagner's operas may be, and actually are, played in the concert hall as instrumental compositions without any loss of effect. This shows that no real union between poetry and music exists in these works; for it is not possible to divorce the music from the words and the dramatic plot where there is a real unity, as in Mozart's *Don Giovanni,* Verdi's *La Traviata,* Monteverde's *Orfeo* or Gluck's *Alceste.* Why Wagner had thus to find and elaborate a fiction to frame and set off his music is a subject for a critical investigation that would be out of place in this book.

W.J. Turner
Music — A Short History
95

The devotion aroused in some people by Wagner's music is different in kind from that aroused by any other composer's. It is like being in love: a kind of madness, a kind of worship, an irrational commitment yet abandonment which, among other things, dissolves the critical faculty. The best-known hatchet man in contemporary British journalism, Bernard Levin, has poured out his adoration over a whole page of the *New Statesman*. After a Promenade concert in the mid-sixties which concluded with the third act of *Götterdämmerung* the young audience cheered for half an hour and then, when the performers finally went home and the lights of the Albert Hall were switched off, carried on cheering in the dark.

The equal and opposite reaction is just as familiar: the militant advocacy is equalled by a militant dislike. Wagner in his lifetime had more, and more bitter, personal enemies than any great composer has ever had, and his music can provoke a hostility not merely greater than any other but, again, different in kind. People who would consider that to condemn the music of any other such famous composer as bad would be foolish if the word were meant aesthetically and meaningless if meant morally do not hesitate to apply it to Wagner's in both senses. His music is denounced, as is no other, in moral terms: it is 'immoral', 'corrupting', 'poisonous', 'degenerate'. The notion that there is something inherently evil in it, a notion as old as the music itself, received its greatest boost from Hitler's worship of Wagner, and the composer's subsequent association with Nazism. To this day there are many people who think there is something fascist in the music.

Here, then, we have a music that gets at people — not everyone, of course, but a remarkable number — in a unique way: gets under their skins, stirs passions that no other music touches, and draws reactions which, whether favourable or unfavourable, are essentially immoderate. 'Prejudice', to quote *Grove's Dictionary of Music*, 'affects judgement of Wagner more than that of almost any other composer.' This fact has been notorious for a hundred years, but it has never, so far as I know, been explained. Yet I think it can be explained.

96

The key is this: Wagner gives expression to things which in the rest of us, and in the rest of art, are unconscious because they are repressed. Modern psychology has familiarised us with the idea — and convinced most of us of its truth — that in the process of growing up and developing independent personalities, and learning to live in society, we have to subordinate some of our most powerful instinctual desires, especially erotic and aggressive ones — for instance passionate sexual feeling towards parents and siblings, or the urge to attack and destroy those on whom we are emotionally dependent — so that these are driven underground, below the level of consciousness, and kept there at the cost of some strain, as a result of which they remain charged with a high emotional voltage. Most of the really important taboos in our society, such as the incest taboo, relate to them. This repression, this inner conflict, is inseparable from living, and is part of the personality of each one of us. I believe that it is from, and to, this level of the personality that Wagner's music speaks.

I cannot prove this, because the emotional content of music is not expressible in words, but from what *is* expressed in words — the texts of the operas and, quite separately, Wagner's prose writings — evidence rises up in abundance to support it. Let us look first at the operas. Their subject matter is, to a remarkable degree, the subject matter of depth psychology. Even today audiences would be inexpressibly shocked if the first act of a new drama were to consist of a prolonged, passionate love scene between brother and sister which culminated in sexual intercourse as soon as the curtain was down. Yet this is the first act of *Die Walküre*. And in the second act it is openly and explicitly approved. Wotan says:

> What wrong
> Did these two do
> When spring united them in love?

And when Fricka (who, let us not forget, is the goddess of marriage) cries out:

My heart shudders,
My brain reels:
Marital intercourse
Between brother and sister!
When did anyone live to see it:
Brother and sister *physically* lovers?

Wotan replies:

You have lived to see it today.
Learn from this
That things can ordain themselves
Though they never happened before.
That these two love each other
Is obvious to you.
Listen to some honest advice:
Smile on their love, and bless
Siegmund and Sieglinde's union.
Their sweet joy
Will reward you for your blessing.

And a moment later, in words which convince us, as so often, that the voice of Wagner is speaking through Wotan:

You only want to understand,
Always, what you are used to:
My mind is reaching out towards
Things that have never happened.

Bryan Magee
Aspects of Wagner

That an opera reveals the psychology of its composer is not, of course, prejudicial to its being a great opera. There are a number of discerning critics who have seen in Wagner's work aspects of his psychological make-up. But it is a characteristic of Puccini's psychology that it is self-destructive, claustrophobic and trivialising. He had evidently concluded that it was difficult enough to make a sound musical structure, properly alternating lively and solemn melodies, solo and ensemble situations, without bothering overmuch about meaning. In 1889 in a Milan theatre he saw a performance of Sardou's melodrama, *Tosca*, and, though he knew only a few words of French, when he heard that Franchetti was thinking of making an opera out of the play, he seized the libretto for himself. Puccini worked hard at the construction of the 'Te Deum' scene, the torture of Cavaradossi, and the final leap, until everything added up to an evening of 'real theatre'. In *Tosca* he has managed to make a struggle for political and personal freedom into an opportunity for delicious singing and melodramatic twists. What was supremely important for Beethoven has become simply a piece of theatrical business. Again, when he saw an American play in London in 1900, though he understood very little of the dialogue he knew at once that *Madama Butterfly* would offer him just the right opportunities for his kind of opera. And, though this opera was a total fiasco at its first performance in Milan in 1904, he was quite right. It does have all the elements of popular art. From the second production in Brescia three months later it has held its place in the repertory of every opera house. But for those who ask such questions a short answer can be given to 'What is this opera about?' Indeed the only appropriate question at the close of *Butterfly* is 'Did you cry?'

Hamish Swanson
In Defence of Opera

Those who were present at the performance of Puccini's opera *Tosca*, were little prepared for the revolting effects produced by musically illustrating the torture and murder scenes of Sardou's play. The alliance of a pure art with scenes so essentially brutal and demoralising . . . produced a feeling of nausea. There may be some who will find entertainment in this sensation, but all true lovers of the gentle art must deplore with myself its being so prostituted. What has music to do with a lustful man chasing a defenceless woman or the dying kicks of a murdered scoundrel? It seemed an odd form of amusement to place before a presumably refined and cultured audience, and should this opera prove popular it will scarcely indicate a healthy or creditable taste.

London newspaper
13 July 1900

Tosca San Francisco Opera, 1961

One must remember that *Tosca* is very often the Cinderella — the last opera of the season in a big opera house. This is because it is thought to be an 'easy' opera; there are in effect only three principals — Tosca, Cavaradossi and Scarpia. Looked at from the point of view of an overworked producer under great pressure, 90 per cent of the battle obviously lies in the principals knowing the work — the other participants amount only to the first-act chorus (some rehearsal needed here), the second-act choir (offstage thank God) and the third-act execution squad (no problem, they don't sing . . .). Alas, it is thus that fatal errors, hideous disasters, are engendered. On this particular occasion that innocuous firing squad was composed of hurriedly enlisted and highly enthusiastic college boys from the local campus, totally ignorant of the story and constantly worrying the producer with their 'When do we come on? What do we do?' His answer was an invariable, 'Wait, wait — I'm working with the principals.' In the end, a combination of illness and a desperately tight schedule led to the cancellation of the dress rehearsal and the appearance on the opening night of the execution squad itself only five minutes after their first and only consultation with the
100

producer. He was still in a hurry, but felt he had given them enough to go on — 'OK, boys. When the stage manager cues you, slow-march in, wait until the officer lowers his sword, then shoot.' 'But how do we get off?' 'Oh — well, exit with the principals.' (This is the standard American instruction for minor characters, servants, etc.)

The audience, therefore, saw the following: a group of soldiers marched on to the stage, but stopped dead in its tracks at the sight of *two* people, not one as they assumed — a man and a woman both looking extremely alarmed. When they pointed their hesitant rifles at the man, he at first drew himself up, looking noble and resigned, but then started giving inexplicable conspiratorial sidelong glances at the woman . . . they pointed them at her, but she made a series of violently negative gestures — but then what else would she do if she was about to be shot? Should they, perhaps, shoot them both? But then they would hardly be standing so far apart — anyway the opera was called *Tosca,* it was evidently tragic, the enormous woman on stage was presumably Tosca herself, solemn funeral music was playing, the officer was raising his sword . . . .

Thus it happened. By a perfectly sensible process of logical deduction they *shot Tosca instead of Cavaradossi.* To their amazement they then saw the man, some twenty yards away, fall lifeless to the ground while the person they *had* shot rushed over to him crying (we must remember this was in a vivid American translation), 'Come on, baby, get up, we gotta go.' What could they do? They had shot one of the principals — though admittedly the wrong one — and their next instruction was '*Exit with the principals.*' In disbelief they watched as, first, Spoletta and his minions burst on to the stage and Tosca — could it be true? took up her position on top of the battlements. She jumped, and there was only one thing for it — as the curtain slowly descended the whole firing-squad threw themselves after her . . . .

Hugh Vickers
Great Operatic Disasters
101

I want to tell you one of the most amusing experiences I have ever had in an opera house. Sir Thomas Beecham was rehearsing Chaliapin in *Don Quichotte* of Massenet, in the death scene. Don Quichotte is dying in a forest, propped up against a tree. In his delirium he has a vision of his beloved Dulcinée. The voice of Dulcinée is heard from offstage, the last sound of the earthly world that Don Quichotte ever hears. At this rehearsal the young girl who was singing the part of Dulcinée came in too late on three occasions, so Beecham called her up to the footlights. 'My dear Miss Nelis, three times Mr Chaliapin has died with the most affecting realism; three times you have come in too late. Why?'

The poor girl was trembling and could hardly speak. She tried to make excuses for herself: 'Oh, Sir Thomas, it is n-n-not my f-fault.'

'And *whose* fault do you think it is?'

'It is not your fault, Sir Thomas. I think it is Mr Chaliapin's fault. He dies too soon.'

Beecham made this historic reply: 'My dear Miss Nelis, no opera singer ever dies too soon!'

Neville Cardus
Conversations with Cardus

The following is an extract from a synopsis of *Carmen*, thoughtfully provided some years ago by the Paris Opera for the benefit of its English and American patrons:

Carmen is a cigar-makeress from a tabago factory who loves with Don José of the mounting guard. Carmen takes a flower from her corsets and lances it to Don José (Duet: 'Talk me of my mother'). There is a noise inside the tabago factory and the revolting cigar-makeresses bursts into the stage.

102

Carmen is arrested and Don José is ordered to mounting guard her but Carmen subduces him and he lets her escape.

ACT 2 The Tavern. Carmen, Frasquita, Mercedes, Zuniga, Morales. Carmen's aria ('the sistrums are tinkling'). Enter Escamillio, a balls-fighter. Enter two smugglers (Duet: 'We have in mind a business') but Carmen refuses to penetrate because Don José has liberated from prison. He just now arrives (Aria: 'Slop, here who comes!') but hear are the bugles singing his retreat. Don José will leave and draws his sword. Called by Carmen shrieks the two smugglers interfere with her but Don José is bound to dessert, he will follow into them (Final chorus: 'Opening sky wandering life'). . . .

AXT 4 a place in Seville. Procession of balls-fighters, the roaring of the balls heard in the arena. Escamillio enters, (Aria and chorus: 'Toreador, toreador. All hail the balls of a Toreador.') Enter Don José (Aria: 'I do not threaten, I besooch you.') but Carmen repels himwants to join with Escamillio now chaired by the crowd. Don José stabbs her (Aria: 'Oh rupture, rupture, you may arrest me, I did kill der') he sings 'Oh my beautiful Carmen, my subductive Carmen. . . .'

John Julius Norwich
A Christmas Cracker

The composer of *Carmen* is nowhere deep; his passionateness is all on the surface, and the general effect of the work is artificial and insincere. Of melody, as the term is generally understood, there is but little. The air of the Toreador is the only bit of 'tune' in the opera, and this . . . scarcely rises above the vulgarity of Offenbach. The orchestration is in the Wagnerian school, though it lacks the richness and the flow of Wagner, and at times is so broken up and elaborated as to confuse by its fragmentary effect, rarely supporting

103

the voice, but nearly always at odds with it. Bizet aimed at originality, and he undoubtedly obtained it, but he obtained monotony at the same time.

Boston *Gazette*
5 January 1879

Readers will by now have begun to suspect that if there are any villains in this collection most are culled from the ranks of the critics. 'The men who have failed', Disraeli called them but, having been one myself, I am in a position to tell you there is someone even worse than a critic — a critic who is proved wrong.

History has now passed its own verdict on Carmen, *and thus on the gentleman from the Boston* Gazette. *It is my belief that it will take a similar view of the roughshod prose which follows:*

Sondheim

At the climax of the evening the chorus points wildly at the audience and accuses it of adopting, only rather less successfully, the same methods as Sweeney Todd. This accusation is, like a great deal else in the musical, pretentious and fatuous. Mass-murderers we may all be in *some* sense, and in other circumstances we would be prepared to listen to the charge.

Sweeney Todd the musical is, if one can imagine such a thing, a tissue of bullshit from start to finish. Don't be deceived by the talk of Sweeney Todd serving a dark and a hungry God. God is dragged in by the heels, kicking and screaming for the sake of a rhyme. The motivation of the barber, even were it successfully established, is matched by the amorality of Mrs Lovett, emotiveless malignity which is more effective on stage because it is less pretentiously got up. Mrs Lovett couldn't give a damn about the barber's victims. Nor could Stephen Sondheim and nor could Hal Prince. If they didn't pretend to care one would leave the musical feeling, well, that was a massively toneless exercise, but never mind. The pretentiousness has been introduced in an attempt to keep down the tastelessness, in rather the same way as people put goats into graveyards in order to keep down the weeds. The result is that one emerges with the sensation of having been dishonestly handled.

Victorian melodrama was not dishonest in this way. Melodrama provided a crudely expressed, but substantially accurate, account of the seamy side of Victorian life. Those poisoners, those deportations, those repentances were real. By contrast, the psychology at Drury Lane is a sham. These lyrics are bogus and painfully contrived. These rhymes are the worst in London.

Sheila Hancock, as Mrs Lovett, brings a considerable comic presence to the stage, and manages to maintain her character's tone of voice while singing. This is not a common gift, particularly with taxing music of this kind. One feels that the show owes a great deal to the familiar and friendly personality which Miss Hancock brings with her.

As for Denis Quilley in the title role, he made one mistake only — but that was the mistake of accepting the part. The effect in New York was the same — the actor was the prisoner of the role and the victim of the production. It is splendid to see Mr Quilley back in the West End. It would be splendider

105

still to see him on the classical stage, or in something — for God's sake — worth watching.

James Fenton
Sunday Times, 6 July 1980

Last year I gave several lectures on 'Intelligence and the Appreciation of Music among Animals'. Today I am going to speak to you about 'Intelligence and the Appreciation of Music among Critics.' The subject is very similar.

Erik Satie

A conversation between two people unhappily thrown together at a party by a hostess who know that both of them have a modest collection of LPs.

A: Were you at Winkelski's recital on Tuesday?
B: Indeed I was. What did you think of the B minor?
A: I wasn't too impressed. I think he's much more at home with the E flat.
A: Oh, really! Surely Richter is the man for that?
B: Yes and no. He always plays the Allegro too fast for my liking and could give it a shade more rubato.
A: Winkelski has a wonderful ear for detail in the B minor.
B: He has a firm touch but lacks variety.
A: And tends to ignore the composer's dynamic markings.
B: He is more at home in music of a deeper chromatic hue.
A: Like the Brahms 2.
B: Exactly.

You can sense from the above that neither has the faintest idea what the other really means (or what he means himself, for that matter) but that the conversation moves along easily
106

like detergent froth on a river. They can now proceed to go through a long list of composers and performers, casting generalised aspersions on the results of years of study and practise or occasionally granting mild approbation.

You can tell that they are not professional critics. If they were the conversation would go more like this:

A: Were you at the Festival Hall on Tuesday?
B: I'm afraid so. Absolute mess in the B minor.
A: Complete mess — he ought to stick to Liszt.
B: They wanted him to do the E flat but he wouldn't.
A: Clot.
B: Couldn't get a bloody coffee in the interval.
A: What a putrid waste of time. See you at Lord's tomorrow?

Peter Gammond
Bluff Your Way in Music

Until I reached the age of 12 I had absolutely no idea what I wanted to be when I grew up. Then I went to my first concert. It was at the Hornsey Town Hall, North London, the orchestra was the London Philharmonic and the conductor was a Rumanian named Sergiu Celibidache. From the very moment this imposing, tall, dynamic man walked out on to the platform, stepped on to the rostrum, and raised two expressive hands — one bearing a slender white baton — I knew what I wanted to be. I wanted to be like him . . . I wanted to be a conductor. One hundred and ten musicians at my total command. An imperceptible nod at the percussion would produce a muffled roll on the timpani, a finger to the lips and the strings would hush to a trembling whisper, sweep down with the right hand and the whole orchestra would crash out a fortissimo chord with the precision of a machine. Then the end of the symphony. A roar of applause from the packed hall, I raise my hands palms upwards and the orchestra obediently stands up, and as I slowly turn and bow the applause swells to a mighty cheer. Well, anyway, that's what happened with Celibidache.

For the next year, standing on a chair in the living-room while the 78s spun on the radiogram, I conducted. Two hours every evening, four hours at weekends. I learned the music by listening to the records, and by the end of the year I had total recall of at least a dozen major symphonic works. Then, just as suddenly as I had embraced my new profession, I abandoned it. It was on the day that a well-meaning friend presented me with an orchestral score. Did all conductors, I asked in the dawn of fearful dread, use one of these? My companion assured me that this was certainly the case. No one could possibly become a conductor without being able to tell at a glance from the mass of bewildering dots, lines and curves exactly what the music ought to sound like. One had to be able to read music as one would a book, and hear every note just from looking at the page. Well, of course, that was that. The following day I decided to be a concert pianist — they had only two lines of music to read!

Since those early days, perhaps in compensation for my total ignorance in the one area vital to the budding maestro, I have expanded my knowledge in all the other less important aspects of conducting, and I now offer a modest selection of 'do's' and 'don'ts' essential to those who can read a score when facing the Cerberus of the musical world, the orchestra.

Crushing the Soloist

All good soloists who come along to play a concerto with you will have firm ideas of exactly how the piece should go, and if you are not careful they will immediately relegate you to the role of mere accompanist, even talking directly to the players as if you weren't there. Put a stop to this at once by beginning the work either very fast or very slow. When the soloist complains it's too quick, slightly raise your eyebrows and say something like: 'That's the way we always do it, but I can take it slower if it's too much for you.' If the complaint is that the tempo is dragging, the reply becomes: 'I don't think the music has much chance to make its point if we tear away like that.' Each time an orchestral introduction ends and the soloist is about to play, turn to him with staring eyes and an exaggerated nod of the head, as if without your help he would have no idea of when to begin playing. The most devastating put-down of any soloist I know was accomplished by the splendid tyrant Sir Thomas Beecham when rehearsing the Delius Piano Concerto with his wife Betty. It was not a happy event and Lady Beecham made many mistakes. When the rehearsal was over, and she left the platform, the hall attendant asked whether or not the piano should be moved before they began the next work; 'Don't worry,' crowed Sir Thomas, 'I expect it will slink off by itself!'

Maximising the Applause

Make the orchestra stand immediately a work is over. This is essential to satisfy their democratic instincts, and if you get it over at the outset the applause will appear to be as much for the composer as for them. Then leave the rostrum and wait in the wings for at least a minute before returning to grab the glory of a solo bow. One recall like this is worth half a dozen rapid, greedy rushes to and fro; it adds great dignity and hints at personal exhaustion after the overwhelming experience you have been so generous to provide. 'Bleeding' or 'milking'

109

applause is an exact art and should not be undertaken by the tyro. The finest example on record is that of a famous American conductor and pianist, who is also a composer of serious and lighter music, who was conducting a performance of a concerto played by another conductor and pianist from the USA. At the end there was a big reception, and the conductor turned to the pianist and said: 'Go on to the platform and take a bow alone.' The pianist demurred. 'Go on,' urged the conductor, 'you played the piece, you deserve the appreciation.' The pianist returned to the platform to an even greater storm of clapping. The moment he came off the stage, the conductor gripped him fiercely on the shoulder and hissed intently in his ear: 'Right. Now *drag me on*!'

Too Little is Better than Too Much

Baton or stick technique could fill a book. Some conductors, like Stokowski, have done without one but this is not to be recommended — after all, in the last resort, every other player (except the pianist) has a weapon of some kind, so why shouldn't you. Use a fair-sized stick (not too big, or they'll think you come from another age and are about 90) and a very small beat most of the time. This both conserves your energy for the big moments and at the same time gives you an excuse when things go wrong, as you can blame the players for not following your beat, the uncertainty of which would be noticeable if most of your gestures were on the large side. Leonard Bernstein may look terrific throwing himself all over the platform but remember he knows exactly where to put his stick. Others, less experienced, have been known to spear the leader's hand, or even their own eye, though for the most spectacular casualty we have to go back as far as 1687, when one of the earliest baton-wielders, the composer Jean-Baptiste Lully, was conducting his own *Te Deum.* Beating time by banging a stick on the floor, poor Lully missed, brought down the stick on his foot, and died a few weeks later after gangrene set in.

110

Ignore the excellent advice above, from composer Richard Strauss, at your peril. The orchestra is your greatest enemy. They all know more than many conductors do, and most of them would like to be where you are. Quite honestly, the best advice I can give you is never to mix it with them if a confrontation can be avoided; you will almost always come off worse. A French composer and conductor who was rehearsing a difficult modern work of his own with a British orchestra wasn't satisfied with the way a certain woodwind passage was being interpreted.

'No, no,' he said irritably, 'not like that, like this . . .' And he sang: 'La-la . . . lalala . . . laaa, la, la!'

'Ah,' said the musician, also singing, 'you mean, la-la . . . lalala . . . laaa, la, la?'

'Yes,' beamed the conductor, 'that's it.'

There was an eloquent pause, and then came the *coup de grâce.* 'Good,' said the clarinettist, 'Now we've established we can both sing it, who's going to play it?'

As the years go on most fiery young conductors are tamed by the orchestra and philosophically mellow into age. An orchestral player, who had conducted a concert for the very first time, bumped into one of the greatest of all the conductors, Hans Richter.

'How did it go?' asked the old man.

'Oh, very well, maestro,' came the answer. 'It was really much easier than I thought.'

'I know, I know,' said Richter. 'So I beg you, please don't give us away!'

Coda

Two years ago I was actually given the chance to conduct a real orchestra for a big charity concert at the Albert Hall. The orchestra was the Royal Philharmonic and the piece one of the easiest in the repertoire, Vaughan Williams's arrangement

111

of 'Greensleeves'. It begins with a slow, lovely, and rather free-tempo flute solo. How should I beat it? After agonising for days I found myself at rehearsal, facing the talented and beautiful principal flautist, Susan Milan. My nerve broke. 'Would you,' I asked, 'play it exactly as you think it ought to go, and then I'll bring in the orchestra when you've finished?' Miss Milan smiled with infinite understanding and then, as must have happened so many times before, did my job for me.

Robin Ray
Preview, 1978

When I am with composers, I say I am a conductor. When I am with conductors, I say I am a composer.

Leonard Bernstein
The World in Vogue, 1963

Oscar Levant *about* **Leonard Bernstein**:

He uses music as an accompaniment to his conducting.

The Memoirs of an Amnesiac, 1965

Legends about orchestral conductors are many, for their authoritative (even supreme) position, though fully understood by musicians and the musically-minded, is apt to be misinterpreted by that larger and less discerning world which boasts many millions unversed in the art's intricacies.

For the sake of my argument it can be assumed that

Beethoven is a household word: a world figure, like Napoleon or Shakespeare, Julius Caesar or even (for the nonce) Primo Carnera — that lately deposed champion of fisticuffs. But whereas there may be millions of the uninitiated who know the pseudo title if not the music of Beethoven's 'Moonlight' Sonata, there are relatively but a few acquainted with his symphonies and still fewer able to appreciate any sustained argument concerning the merits or demerits of a conductor's *interpretation* of those symphonies.

For the word 'interpretation', as applied to the conductor of an orchestra, conveys to many folk a meaning so ambiguous as to be almost unintelligible. They find it difficult to appreciate the finer points of an art that, in its technique, is intimately bound up with some kind of mysterious silence, while, on the contrary, the contribution of the players themselves is one of rich and glowing sounds. And so, to them, the conductor is little more than a 'time-beater'; his baton but a modern development of that roll of parchment which did rough and ready service in those days of long ago when orchestral music was practically unknown.

Yet without the silent gestures, the wave of the arm or the quick exchange of glances between conductor and instrumentalist, the art of interpretation as applied to orchestral music would be in sorry plight. The actual time-beating is nothing more than elementary technique, acquired by instinct or study, incorporated in the course of time as an integral part of the conductor's equipment, and then reproduced by him quite automatically. And until he has mastered the technique of the baton as a directing agency he will never be able to interpret music with any skill or feeling, for every technical shortcoming is noticed immediately by the instrumentalists supposedly under his control: a feeling of uncertainty will prevail and thereby prevent anything in the nature of stylism or the reproduction of the inner spirit of the music.

The conductor, therefore, learns his technique only to forget it — a palpable truism that applies here as much as it does to all human endeavour. His sole object is to concentrate on the artistic side of the performance and to recreate in living sounds what the composer has put so inspiredly on paper.

Julius Harrison
The Orchestra and Orchestral Music

It seems fitting that the earliest-born of the great conductors to record was Arthur Nikisch, the idol of his day, the conductor who was to his generation what Toscanini and Furtwängler were to the period after World War I. When we hear the old Nikisch recordings, and he made quite a few, we are listening to the work of a man born in 1855. (André Messager, born two years before Nikisch, also recorded; but Messager, an able operatic conductor, was not one of the great ones and lives today only by his charming stage works.) And when we listen to the Nikisch recordings we also are listening to the work of a man who achieved the respect and the admiration of virtually every musician who ever came into contact with him. Unlike so many great conductors, Nikisch was easygoing and understanding, and he had no enemies. Not an especially learned man — Carl Flesch called him 'intellectually primitive' — he read nothing, cared only for music, cards, women and company. Nevertheless he was a good practical psychologist. His years as a violinist in many orchestras had given him an insight into the mental workings of orchestral players, and he automatically got on their right side. Orchestras loved him and would do anything for him. Nobody ever saw him lose his temper. His politeness never failed him, and his harshest words to an orchestra were 'Excuse me, gentlemen, but . . .' or 'Will you kindly . . .' The first time Lotte Lehmann sang under his baton, as Freia in *Das Rheingold*, she was nervous and let out a shriek. Nikisch called her to the footlights. 'You're a beginner, I hear. But you mustn't be so terribly frightened. Just take a good look at me. Do I look as bad as all that? Well, then, let's try again.'

Fritz Busch at one time played in the Colonne Orchestra and Nikisch came as a guest conductor. At the first rehearsal, wrote Busch, he strode forth and beamed to the horns and winds on his way to the podium 'with such charm that when he stepped up on the conductor's rostrum, the whole orchestra was already on its feet and had broken out into enthusiastic applause'. Nikisch took his time. He removed his kid gloves. He said that it was the dream of his life to conduct this famous orchestra. (He said this to all orchestras.) Suddenly his eye lit on an old viola player. 'Schulze, what are *you* doing here? I had no idea you had landed in this beautiful city. Do you remember how we played the *Bergsymphonie* under Liszt at Magdeburg?' Schulze indeed remembered, and immediately resolved that with *this* conductor he would use the whole length of his bow instead of the half he gave other conductors. By this time the orchestra would have died for Nikisch. Busch ended up calling him 'the born guest conductor, an improviser of genius'.

And in 1905 a member of the London Symphony Orchestra described the impact that Nikisch could make on musicians. The orchestra was in the midst of preparations for a festival and had been working nine hours a day. On this particular evening, it had had a morning rehearsal, an afternoon concert, and was scheduled for the first Nikisch rehearsal at seven. Tchaikovsky's Fifth Symphony (a Nikisch speciality) was the work, and the men were tired and sullen. But: 'Before we had been playing five minutes we were deeply interested and, later, when we came to the big fortissimos we not only played like fiends but forgot we were tired.' At the end of the first movement the orchestra rose and yelled its appreciation. 'The weird part of it all was that we played the symphony through — with scarcely a word of direction from Herr Nikisch — quite differently from our several previous performances of the same work. He simply *looked* at us, often scarcely moving his baton, and we played as those possessed.'

For many years Nikisch pondered the kind of men who played for him. He came to a conclusion that a player's psyche depended upon the kind of instrument he played. Clarinettists as a species, he maintained, are inclined to be sentimental and must be addressed with infinite gentleness. Violists or any of the higher brass instruments are calm and good-humoured. Therefore with them a humorous or even slightly rude approach works best. Oboists and bassoonists are different. They have to blow into a narrow reed in such a manner that a great amount of air remains stored in the chest, to be released cautiously and gradually. This makes the blood rise to the brain and makes them so nervous they can be addressed only with the greatest tact. All these opinions Nikisch would expound with a straight face, but presumably with a twinkle in his own psyche.

A small man with a neatly trimmed, pointed beard, a dandy who affected an enormous mop of hair even before Paderewski floated through the skies with his aureole, a man who liked hand-made shirts with enormous collars and cuffs (these cuffs set off his tiny white hands and made them look even smaller), Nikisch seemed to have mesmeric powers over an orchestra. 'Mesmeric' is the one word that crops up again and again in relation to Nikisch, and musicians all over Europe and America would go around telling everybody that they 'felt unlike themselves' when Nikisch conducted. Apparently he had that trait from the beginning. He had started as a piano prodigy from Hungary who scared people with his natural aptitude for music. At the age of 7, for example, he heard the *William Tell* and *Barber of Seville* overtures for the first time, then went home and wrote them out from memory; and at 8 he had made his debut as a pianist. (He kept up his piano technique all his life, and was fond of accompanying singers in concert, including the great Elena Gerhardt.) At the age of 11 he was in the Vienna Conservatory, and after graduating became a violinist in the Vienna Court Orchestra, where he played under such conductors as Brahms, Wagner, Herbeck and Dessoff. His own conducting career had an unusually rapid advancement. In 1878 he made his début in Leipzig with an operetta named *Jeanne, Jeannette, Jeanetton.* A few

116

months later, at the age of 23, he was busy conducting *Die Walküre* and *Tannhäuser;* and at 24, on the retirement of Josef Sucher, he became first conductor of the Leipzig Opera, where he remained for eleven years.

Some of his effects Nikisch achieved by evolving a new kind of baton technique. Nikisch probably was the first to guide the baton with fingers and wrist rather than fist and arm. This led to a more flexible beat and subtlety of expression. The baton seemed part of Nikisch's hand, an extension of his fingers. He used a long, thin, light stick and developed his left hand far more than any previous conductor had done. It was said of him that his left hand was never seen reflecting his right. When he wanted a legato, a horizontal, dragging motion of the baton was enough to do the job. Adrian Boult, who studied in Leipzig and was in constant attendance at the Nikisch rehearsals and performances, has written that Nikisch 'made his stick say more than any other conductor that I have ever seen. His power of expression was so intense that one felt it would be quite impossible, for instance, to play staccato when Nikisch was showing a legato.' Boult describes Nikisch as holding the baton with two fingers and thumb, the fingers separated by about a finger's width, the thumb exactly opposite the space between them. Among other innovations of Nikisch was the device of beating in advance, giving the note value a fraction of a second early. This was adopted by Furtwängler (as, indeed, he adopted many things from Nikisch). Nikisch almost always conducted from memory, although he invariably had a score before him. 'I do not think you can conduct well,' he said, 'unless you know a work by heart or almost by heart.'

No other conductor could get such a sound from an orchestra. When Harold Bauer played the Schumann Piano Concerto with Nikisch his heart sank, for 'no soloist — I least of all — could hope to equal the beauty of sound that he conjured from the orchestra in the opening theme.' Nikisch could get beauty of sound from any orchestra, even one he had never worked with before. When he conducted at La Scala he

117

complimented Toscanini on the fine quality of the orchestra. Toscanini would have none of it. 'My dear, I happen to know this orchestra very well. I am the conductor of this orchestra. It is a bad orchestra. You are a good conductor.' Richard Strauss said that Nikisch had 'the ability to get a sound out of the orchestra which we others do not possess'. Furtwängler echoed Strauss: 'Nikisch had precisely the capacity to make an orchestra sing.' Nikisch would step in front of an orchestra, and the young Furtwängler would stay awake nights trying to figure out 'why every orchestra sounded so changed under the simple beats of Arthur Nikisch; why the winds played without their usual exaggerated sforzati, the strings with a singing legato, and the sound of the brass fused with the other instruments, while the general tone of the orchestra acquired a warmth which it did not have with other conductors.'

Harold C. Schonberg
The Great Conductors

Unwanted Notes

At the Ministry of Defence, where the search is on for cuts in the Armed Forces, a rather pointed story is circulating about the company chairman who gave his work study consultant an unwanted concert ticket and received, the next day, the following memo:

a) For considerable periods the four oboe players had nothing to do. The number should be reduced, and their work spread over the whole orchestra, thus eliminating peaks of inactivity.

b) All twelve violins were playing identical notes. This seems unnecessary duplication, and the staff of this section should be drastically cut.

The playing of the demi-quavers, concluded the consultant,

118

was an 'excessive refinement' absorbing much effort. All notes should therefore be rounded up to the nearest semi-quaver; then it should be possible to use 'trainees and low-grade operators'.

Daily Telegraph
Tuesday, 8 May 1984

Having already spoken of this question of deputies in Chapter XVIII, it might be of interest if I explained the whole situation and how it was eventually dealt with. The members of the Queen's Hall Orchestra had accepted their individual contracts for a 150 concerts per season but had the right to send deputies in case of illness or when they were offered outside engagements. The former was reasonable enough; but the latter simply meant that when they were offered jobs at a higher fee than that which they received for being at Queen's Hall they took these jobs, sent a deputy at a lower figure, and 'kept the change'. It obviously paid them.

Had it only occurred in one or two isolated cases nothing might have been said; but to find on a Monday morning that my orchestra contained seventy to eighty new faces — people I had never seen before in many instances — was beyond a joke. I had to endure the same thing during the run of *The Lady Slavey*. I appointed a double-bass player whom I never saw again after the opening — and yet the show ran for a hundred nights.

So that it is not surprising that in 1904 I took up a definite position, Robert Newman (as usual) backing me up. The way he dealt with the situation was thoroughly characteristic. As I have already pointed out, he was a man of few words. Neither would he ever go on to the platform and make a speech to the orchestra. Instead he wrote down on a piece of paper what he wanted to say, never wasting a word, and proceeded to *read* what he had written. On this occasion he strode on to the platform in his customary businesslike manner, halted, held up the paper, and read thus: 'Gentlemen, in future there will be *no* deputies! . . . *Good* morning!' With which he strode off.

There was no argument about it. Nothing was said to either of us, we simply found that about forty members had resigned and that we were faced with the task of replacing them. This we quickly did. Those forty players then formed an orchestra of their own which they called the London Symphony Orchestra. So that I was directly the cause of the formation of that well-known body of musicians who gave their first concert on 9 June 1904, Richter being their principal conductor until 1911. Everybody seems to have conducted them: Nikisch, Safonov, Arbos, Koussevitsky, Steinbach, Mengelberg, Furtwängler, Coates. My action may have seemed high-handed at the time, but it at least provided London with two permanent orchestras of first-rate quality instead of only one.

Henry J. Wood
My Life of Music

I never use a score when conducting my orchestra . . . . Does a lion tamer enter a cage with a book on how to tame a lion?

Dimitri Mitropoulos
22 January 1951

A most entertaining book entitled Orchestra *is devoted almost entirely to the men and women who, day in and day out, here, there and everywhere, in a variety of circumstances and under a variety of conductors actually play the music, and give the performances which we later recall as memorable.*

They are more than entitled to their say in a book like this, and I give a selection of their comments with great pleasure.

There was an article in the papers a while ago about the drinking on the London Symphony tour of Japan. Well, I was on that tour and I didn't see anything much. But, yes, nerves and strain do lead to drinking in orchestras, and nowadays there's a lot of drinking everywhere. Brass players like to drink beer, though I don't care for it. It relaxes them. I used to drink, and I've found that if you enjoy a drink, it's fine. But if you're drinking for a purpose, because you are afraid of the job or the instrument, then it's fatal. It's *fatal.* I know a few who do that, and I've even told them it's fatal. I think I'm entitled to tell them because I'm much older and I've seen bad things happen to players through drink. You can understand how it happens, delays in travelling, boredom in buses and trains and at airports, things go wrong. You can't always be on parade. But drinking before a concert is another matter, that's usually out of fear or nerves. You start doing that, you fall down on the job, and you don't last very long.

William Lang
(Trumpet)

The horn does have a reputation for difficulty, though nowadays you can get working models, you might say, which ensure that all the notes that used to be bad on, say, Alexander horns are easier to get. The tubing has been ironed out and the notes are in the centre, as it were, but in doing this they've somehow made a metal instrument without much character.

121

People playing these horns tend to sound all the same to me. That's my own prejudice, and I find them difficult to play. I like a horn with a bit of a problem that you must work out for yourself.

Facial make-up, mouth and lips and teeth, are important. Sticking-out teeth, or the wrong size, can affect the horn sound. Also thick lips are not always good. You could say get a larger mouthpiece, but there's a limit to size if you want to keep a characteristic sound. But now sound is a matter of personal preference. At one time a horn sound was a horn sound, but now there's so much variation and everyone is right.

Well, I keep on playing the old hand-horn, the natural horn with no valves. It gives you extremely good lip flexibility, and you still have to listen for your notes before you play them, and know exactly where you are going to pitch them. Many young horn players, notably in America, at an early age get a huge American Conn double horn. They know nothing about the beginnings of the horn, the harmonic series is all by-passed. They have a gross four-valve instrument that comes out like a euphonium, or baritone horn, as far as I can hear. And the hand positions are so important, the right hand is not there just to hold the horn up, you have to humour the notes with the right hand. Now, many of these kids achieve a sort of perfection, but it's up the wrong alleyway. There's something missing, because they are ignorant of the real nature of the instrument. So I go on with the old instruments trying to get the essential sound in my head.

Ordinarily, I play on one instrument, though I may change, depending on the music. I have a descant horn for Bach or anything high. It takes some of the misery out of the higher octave, but the danger is that the sound will come out like a bugle. People play on them all the time, which puzzles me, because the sound is not that good. My normal horn I bought in 1948, from Alexander in Germany. It cost me £44 — I'm still playing it. And I've had possibly fifteen other horns since then, which I've tried and discarded. Now the Alexander is really on its last legs, it's clapped out. All the valves leak, there are patches on it, it's thin in the bell. I think if it packs up, I shall have to pack up too.

Alan Civil
(French Horn)

My first entry on my first appearance with the Philharmonia; it was the *Rite of Spring*. The bassoon begins, starting cold, and it's difficult music. If I mess this up, I thought, I'll wreck the performance for everybody. I remember it was as if I'd been living on a diet of molten lead, nerves at the end. And when you come out you are still quivering, you can't switch off. No wonder orchestras are torn by tensions, soured by animosities. The pressure of playing, of making music live! I recall once a secretary got caught in the studio, just as we were about to start a recording session with Karajan. She found herself stranded right in the orchestra, and she said later she had no idea about this sudden generation of electric tension, the fellows she had seen in the office often enough suddenly transformed by the red recording light. And at concerts we look very grand on the platform, all dressed up like elegant gents. Does the audience know that some players are at the last extremity of fright? You might rehearse time and time again, but the danger of going wrong always exists, and the occasion is so important. You are gathering yourself to give a *performance* of great music.

Cecil James
(Bassoon)

It's such an elusive thing, how conductors affect orchestras. Somebody like Stokowski, whom one might be tempted to write off as a silly old fool, staggered on to the rostrum at a venerable age, hardly able to lift a hand. Yet people are riveted by the sight of him, and scared stiff too. He drops a languid hand in a camp gesture, and a tough and cynical brass section lets go with a blazing fortissimo. 'Not together,' he snaps, and the next time it damn well will be together, because that's the way it has to be. And it wasn't a question of being convinced that Stokowski was a great musician. I thought many of the things he did were gross travesties, which perhaps worked in a superficial, glossy way. Maybe that was what he was after, for certain pieces are best presented in that way. I would listen to late Stokowski perform *Scheherazade*, for instance, because that's what it is, nothing more. But I wouldn't care to listen to a Mahler symphony from him, because Mahler can go several layers deeper.

Anthony Pay
(Clarinet)

Tyrannical conductors were pretty much the story forty years ago. Reiner was that way — Oh God, a holy terror. Stokowski also, in a different way, but the stories with that man over the years are pretty bloodcurdling. In those days the union was rather weak. Those old conductors would throw a man out without blinking. Players stood for tantrums and tyranny because there was a great insecurity. You can imagine, during the Depression, with millions out of work and many actually starving, if a man had a job playing twenty-eight weeks a year in a symphony orchestra, he hung on to it whatever happened. Tantrums and nonsense apart, I firmly believe that an orchestra works best under a benevolent dictatorship. You can't have a hundred chiefs. It's just that a conductor must understand the limits of propriety and decency, and in those days many didn't, being both foul-mouthed and sadistic.

But this modern buddy-buddy approach, happy-go-lucky and not making any demands is not good either. This fashionable conducting, jetting around the world, couple of days here and there, what can they give or demand in that time? This is one reason, to my mind, why orchestras are losing personality, the whole thing becoming a homogenised product. You can't blame these men for wanting to take advantage of the extraordinary life offered to them. Fêted, pampered, praised, *and* very highly paid — who can resist that? But it's not good for the orchestra, or for music necessarily.

John de Lancie
(Oboe)

I must say Karajan, and I think Haitink too, really made their names in England, on our orchestras. Karajan was at first little known. They were not keen to let him in, on account of a dubious wartime past. I remember we did a Balakirev symphony with him. He said he wanted something 'like the crack of a whip', and everyone in the orchestra went, 'Now, now, now!' You know, he is a very clever man, he never made that kind of mistake again.

Anonymous musician

The leader of the old Philharmonia told me that when he was leaving the orchestra he went to see Klemperer. He'd done so much with the old man, even played his trio, and he felt some kind of relationship with Klemperer. He was sorry to be leaving. After his last concert he felt he should go and say something. He said, 'Dr Klemperer, after all these years this is my last concert with you . . . .' And Klemperer replied, 'What you want me to do, cry?'

Anonymous musician
125

Beecham did everything with his eyes. Wherever you were sitting you had this wonderful feeling of contact with him — you personally, even at the back of the seconds. But you can sit under the nose of a bad conductor and you get nothing, *nothing* at all.

Beecham hated sharing the platform, and Heifetz of course was no more interested in conductors than Tommy was in soloists, so they didn't get on very well. On one occasion, when they were appearing together at the Festival Hall, Beecham decided on some sabotage. In the cadenza of the concerto, first he had a prolonged fit of coughing, then he produced a tin of cough sweets and spilt them all over the platform.

The last time Beecham conducted us, in Portsmouth, we were doing the overture to *The Magic Flute.* We just rehearsed the chords, a beast for any conductor, then he called a halt. It was Cup Final day, so he had two TV sets of the largest kind wheeled in and we all watched the football game with Tommy. Another time, recording the *Messiah,* he obviously thought the band wasn't happy enough, so he suddenly produced two bottles of Scotch for the coffee-break at 11.15 in the morning. We loved him very much. We knew he was very ill, after that Portsmouth concert, but when I heard he was dead I was nearly in tears. On that day, a Saturday, we had a concert with Fistulari. Now he was a nice man, not a bad musician, but apt to get confused and certainly no Beecham. It was a Tchaikovsky programme at the Festival Hall, all Tommy's pieces. We rehearsed it, and the orchestra was so depressed, doubly so because we were doing Tommy's music with this other fellow. We were going to play one of Grieg's little string pieces, in memory of Tommy. We began rehearsing it with Fistulari, who was one of those showy conductors, lots of waving about. I felt so awful that I phoned the manager after the rehearsal and said we could very well play the Grieg by ourselves, without Fistulari. So that's what we did in the evening. I remember looking round at the wind section, just sitting there, waiting for the little string piece to end, and

126

some had tears running down their faces. The memory of a great thing now finished.

Anonymous musician

The old conductors were brilliant at producing tensions in the orchestra, frightening people. A man like Koussevitsky, he was a nasty bit of work, but a fine musician and a brilliant psychologist, knowing how to dominate and intimidate. He knew also, quite correctly, that if the orchestra really loathed him, yet was frightened of him, he would often get very good performances. I remember playing like an absolute angel for people I hated, through sheer tension and dislike. Very strange. But you had to be convinced of their music-ality. Conductors don't have the power now to sack or intimidate. With our self-governing orchestras, if a man is really unpleasant, and unmusical into the bargain, we kick him out straightaway.

Richard Adeney
(Flute)

Orchestra
Edited by André Previn

Show me an orchestra that likes its conductor and I'll show you a lousy orchestra.

Goddard Lieberson
Quoted by Hubert Kupferberg in
Those Fabulous Philadelphians, 1969

8 May 1964

It is hard to realise that tall, spare, Machiavellian, sinister Mr Lieberson will be honoured by Columbia Records on his twenty-fifth anniversary.

Over the years I have listened to many of the recordings that Mr Lieberson has endorsed; some of them so meretricious that I am amazed that the postal authorities allowed them to be sent through the regular mails.

Choosing a hit record is, admittedly, a difficult assignment, and I can only assume that swarthy, decadent Mr Lieberson was chosen for this job because of his position — which is invariably horizontal.

Apparently it never occurred to those criminally responsible for elevating him to this high office, that a flair and instinct for music was a necessary requisite.

It is tragic to think that one who guides the destiny of a worldwide music organisation should be unable to distinguish between Mozart's 'Jupiter' Symphony and 'Tomorrow Night at the Darktown Strutters' Ball'.

Despite his obvious deficiencies, I can truly say that his entire organisation (to say nothing of me) loves him with the same fervor that is usually reserved for men like Stalin, Hitler and Torquemada.

Groucho Marx
The Groucho Letters

May I add to the correspondence concerning methods of using a record collection in the thought that readers may be interested in my system.

I have a library of over 600 discs and, now that storage space is fully occupied, a few cassettes. Record sleeves are given a small adhesive label (top left-hand corner) which is numbered. Boxes and cassettes each have a different series of numbers with the prefix B or T. Discs and boxes are filed in the storage cabinets in numerical order. Cassettes await a suitable storage arrangement.

Immediately after purchase details of discs and cassettes are entered in a card index kept under composers' names in alphabetical order and showing the relative storage shelf number. Recital records are card-indexed under Recitals with a cross-index under composer's name. Selection of any record from the shelves is simple and rapid.

Our listening method is to decide upon a correct pro-gramme. We never play single record sides or have back-ground music. Concerts (usually lasting a minimum one and a half hours) come under a variety of headings — orchestral, choral, opera, chamber, early music, baroque, recitals. Songs with piano, lute, or guitar are usually included in chamber or recital programmes. Occasionally we have a 'Festival' which means playing, in consecutive concerts, recordings of, say, all the Beethoven string quartets or symphonies or all the Schubert, Bruckner or other symphonies with what we think are appropriate additions to each programme. In addition I keep a diary note of the birthdays of many composers and upon the anniversaries we try to have a suitable concert.

After every evening concert I write the programme in a 'Concert Record Book'! These books I do not destroy and find them most useful in the compilation of programmes and the ensurance of fairly full use of all the record library. These books also provide a good indication of the length of time a stylus has been in use.

A.G.G. O'Brian
Letter to Gramophone, July 1982

Over a period of eighteen years teacher **Mike Edwards** *saved up some priceless comments on music from elementary schoolchildren, publishing them in the March 1975 issue of* Music Journal.

Here are just some of the comments the children made:

Music sung by two people at the same time is called a duel.

I know what a sextet is but I had rather not say.

Caruso was at first an Italian. Then someone heard his voice and said it would go a long way, so he came to America.

A xylophone is an instrument used mainly to illustrate the letter X.

Clarinet reeds are so thin and crackable they are really not good for anything but clarinet reeds.

A tuba is much longer than its name sounds.

Gregory (of the Gregorian Chant) lived from 540 to 604, but I forgot whether it was AC or DC.

Agnus Dei was a woman composer famous for her church music.

Probably the most marvellous fugue was the one between the Hatfields and the McCoys.

Morris dancing is a country survival from the time when people were happy.

Beethoven wrote music even though he was deaf. He was so deaf he wrote loud music. He took long walks in the forest even when everybody was calling him.

Beethoven expired in 1827 and shortly later died from this.

Mozart was a great musician because he practised without someone having to be there to hit him over the head with a hangernade (sic.). He never forgot to practise, and even when he did he was sorry.

Paganini did not have fatness, but just skinny bones.

Handel was half German, half Italian and half English. He was rather large.

Bach is the most famous composer in the world and so is Handel.

J.S. Bach died from 1750 to the present.

Music owes as much to Bach as religion to its founder.

Robert Schumann

Bach we approach with some trepidation. Bach is not really a mere musical commodity at all, but a religion. He is adored by all intellectual virgins (male or female). Like cold showers and hot baths, Bach's music is an almost satisfactory substitute for sex. Its purity grips minds slightly too rarified to be properly religious. It must be listened to, sung and played and discussed with an expression of ineluctable piety. Compared with the music of Bach, Beethoven's and Mozart's efforts are the soiled product of the dirty human hand.

It is possible to like Bach and nothing else — it is even likely. Yet in spite of the clinical and demanding nature of his music it is tremendously popular. If you meet a real Bach addict it would be better to faint or pretend that you have to get home because of the babysitter. Any suggestion that you like other composers just as much, or even more, but can take Bach as good clean fun and enjoy playing his suites for solo cello (in stereo) while you lie in the bath, can earn you a very nasty reputation. You must take Bach seriously or not at all.

Fortunately there is only one remark that is necessary in

connection with Bach in normal conversation and that is, 'Ah ... Bach!' We realise that this is very unhelpful in a way but if you stick to that one remark, with varying inflections, it would seem the safest course to take and covers all emergencies.

One can feel sorry for Bach, privately, for one thing – he has been afflicted with BWV numbers, which we hate deeply and bitterly, great ugly things with not a breath of poetry about them. It is unfair that any composer should be lumbered with such a typographical curse. There is not much that you can say in a critical spirit about his life. As a youth he walked more than 400 miles to hear Buxtehude play the organ (not even standing through a Promenade concert can equal that for musical devotion), but after this initial penance he settled down to a life of hard work, most of it spent at the keyboard and writing an unremitting flood of music, all of it clever and clean. He even worked hard in the evenings but still managed to have twenty children. What else can one say about such a man except 'Ah ... Bach!' The first person who actually said this was his wife.

Peter Gammond
Bluff Your Way in Music

The most prolific composer of all time was Georg Philipp Telemann (1681–1767). His works are in process of being catalogued by a group of German scholars to be published as the *Telemann-Werk-Verzeichnis* by Bärenreiter in Kassel, Germany. This project was begun in 1950 and is still not complete; therefore it is too soon to attempt to give an accurate list of his compositions.

It is known, however, that he composed forty operas, forty passions, over a hundred cantatas, and countless (as yet) orchestral suites and overtures (some estimates make it nearly 600, although a published thematic catalogue lists

132

only 135, of which one is a doubtful attribution), concertos for virtually every melody instrument in existence at that time, hundreds of keyboard works and chamber pieces, etc. No other composer covered so wide a field so prolifically.

The fastest composer? This question has often been asked, but the answer cannot be clear since the question is imprecise. The *consistently* fastest composer must be Schubert who composed over 1,000 works (each of his operas, cycles of songs numbering up to twenty-four individual items, suites of dances for piano or orchestra, and other groups of compositions counting as *one* each) in eighteen years, five months (May 1810 to October 1828). There are many instances in which Schubert would start and finish a work during the course of a single day.

Robert and Celia Dearling and Brian Rust
The Guinness Book of Music Facts and Feats

During a country walk which I took with Schubert in 1821 I asked him if he had ever been in love. Because he showed himself to be so cold and unresponsive toward the fair sex, I had formed the opinion that he disliked women. 'Oh, no,' he replied. 'I loved one with all my heart; and she loved me in return. She was somewhat younger than I, and she sang the soprano solos magnificently and with deep feeling in a Mass I composed. She was not beautiful, and her face was marked with smallpox, but she was good — good to the heart. For three years I hoped to marry her, but I could find no situation, which caused both of us great sorrow. She then married another man, because her parents wished it. I still love her, and since then no other can please me so well or better. The fact is, she was not destined for me.'

Anselm Hüttenbrenner
Quoted by Newman Flower in
Franz Schubert, The Man and His Circle

Among the rank and file of Marmontel's class, there was one about whom his comrades had few illusions. Or rather, they had many, all of them unflattering. Time was to undeceive them markedly to his advantage — to his glory, indeed, and their discomfiture. 'Here you are at last, my boy,' Marmontel would say, as a small, sickly-looking lad came in, generally late. He wore a belted tunic and carried in his hand a kind of cap. Nothing about him suggested the artist, present or future; neither his face, nor his speech, nor his playing. His only remarkable feature was his forehead. He was one of the youngest of the pianists, but by no means one of the best. I remember, in particular, the nervous habit he had of emphasising the strong beats by a kind of panting or raucous breathing. This exaggerated marking of the rhythm was certainly the very last thing of which he could have been accused later on, as a composer, even if it applied to him as a pianist. You will agree with me when you hear his name. He was Claude Debussy. A very reserved, rather sullen boy, he was not popular with his fellow-students.

Camille Bellaigue
Quoted by Leon Vallas in
Claude Debussy — His Life and Works

Next, three love stories, the relationships wildly different, the ends tragic.

134

Robert Schumann

Dear Sir,   Leipzig, 30 June 1839

I should be glad if I could see you today on very important private business. As I may not be able to express myself with sufficient clearness and composure, however, I prefer to send you beforehand a strictly accurate statement in writing.

In September 1837 I made a formal offer of marriage to Fraulein Clara Wieck through her father, Herr Friedrich Wieck, a dealer in musical instruments of this place. Our acquaintance was of long standing, and I had, before taking this step, exchanged a promise of marriage with her. Her father gave me no decisive answer until October of the same year, when he wrote expressing himself as directly opposed to our marriage on the ground of his daughter's small means and my own. I had in my first letter given him a truthful representation of my financial position, fixing my yearly income at about 1,300 talers.

Herr Wieck took his daughter to Vienna that winter, and Clara wrote to me from there in the spring of 1838 to say that her father had given his consent subject to certain conditions. On their return to Leipzig, Herr Wieck paid me a visit in my room without even referring to the matter. I was offended, and thereafter avoided him as much as possible. He, for his part, was irritated by my behaviour, and began openly to oppose our intended union, attempting in every possible way to lower me in the eyes of his daughter and others. With a view to relieving the strained situation, I went to Vienna in September, partly in the hope of mollifying Herr Wieck by my absence, partly to prepare a new existence for Clara and myself. But I found less scope than I had imagined, and returned in April of the present year. Meantime Clara's untiring efforts to win her father's consent were unavailing. He even went so far in his active hostility as to slander me in the most barefaced way. Clara, whose health had suffered by this unnatural behaviour, decided to travel, and went away without her father, though by no means without his consent. This was before my return to Leipzig. She is now in Paris. We began to see that we should never gain our point with Herr Wieck by peaceful methods, and were considering serious measures, when, some weeks ago, to our surprise, Clara received written consent under certain conditions, which I now append. I hope they will not give you a false impression of me. The conditions were:

1. That we should not live in Saxony during his lifetime, but that I should undertake to earn as much elsewhere as I do through editing a musical paper here.
2. That he should keep Clara's money, paying 4 per cent interest, and only paying over the capital five years hence.
3. That I should have the statement of my income, as submitted to him in September, 1837, legally vouched, and place it in the hands of a solicitor chosen by himself.
4. That I should make no attempt to communicate with him verbally or in writing until he so desires.
5. That Clara should give up all claim to inherit anything from him after his death.
6. That we should be married by Michaelmas.

We cannot submit to these conditions, the last excepted, and are therefore determined to have recourse to law.

To leave no stone unturned, I was prevailed upon by Clara to write to him once more in a conciliatory tone. The answer, sent through his wife, was to the effect that he 'wished to have no further dealings' with me.

Yesterday I received from Paris the power of attorney, duly signed by Clara, and viséd by the Saxon embassy. I shall do myself the honour of showing it to you today, if possible, with the request that you will help the brave, faithful girl to the best of your power.

We want the matter settled with all possible dispatch, and are willing to make another peaceable attempt to secure our end if you advise it, and think there is anything to be gained by an interview with Herr Wieck. Failing that, we shall apply to the court, which cannot refuse its consent, as our income is assured.

But I can tell you the rest when I see you. Will you kindly fix a time for the interview, and send me word by the messenger? I ask your services in a noble cause, my dear sir — the reunion of two lovers who have been parted for many years. We look to you for help, and need hardly add a request for strictest secrecy.

May I claim your sympathy for my betrothed as for myself?

Yours faithfully,
Robert Schumann

The morbid symptoms so often recurring in 1852 not only reappeared in 1853, but new ones were added. This was the time of 'table-tipping', which put Schumann into perfect ecstasies, and in every sense of the word, captivated him. Table-tipping agitated many prudent people at that time, going the rounds of the boudoirs and tea parties of nervous ladies, and the studios of otherwise earnest men; but their feelings were different from Schumann's nervous frenzy. While visiting Düsseldorf in May 1853, I one day entered his room, and found him on the sofa reading. To my enquiry as to the subject of his book, he replied in an excited tone, 'Oh! don't you know anything about "table-tipping"?' I laughingly answered, 'Well!' Upon this, his eyes, generally half shut and in-turned, opened wide, the pupils dilated convulsively, and with a peculiar, ghostlike look, he said, slowly and mournfully, 'The tables know all.' When I saw that he was in dead earnest, rather than irritate him I fell into his humour, and he soon grew calm. He then called his second daughter and began to experiment with her aid and a small table, which tapped out the beginning of Beethoven's C minor Symphony. The whole scene struck me with terror; and I well remember that I expressed my distress to acquaintances at the time. He wrote of his experiements to Ferd. Hiller, 25 April 1853: *We tipped the table* yesterday for the first time. Wonderful power! Just think! I asked for the first two measures of the C minor Symphony! It delayed longer than usual with the answer: at last it began, but rather slowly at first. When I said, "But the time is faster, dear table", it hastened to beat the true time. When I asked if it could give the number which *I was thinking of,* it gave it correctly as *three.* We were all filled with wonder.' And to the same, on 29 April, 'We have repeated our experiments in magnetism; we seem surrounded with wonders.'

There were also occasional auricular delusions, which caused him to hear an uninterrupted sound, and in his nervous excitement he really heard it, although there was nothing in the slightest degree approaching a sound. The violinist Ruppert Becker of Frankfort-on-the-Main, who then lived in Düsseldorf, told me that he was at a modest restaurant with Schumann one evening. Suddenly Schumann threw down the paper saying, 'I can read no more; I hear an incessant A.'

The auricular delusions again appeared. He imagined that he heard a tone, which pursued him incessantly, and from which harmonies, indeed, whole compositions, were gradually developed. Spirit voices were heard whispering in his ear, now gentle, now rude and reproachful. They robbed him of sleep for the last two weeks of his wretched existence. One night he rose suddenly, and called for a light, saying that Franz Schubert and Mendelssohn had sent a theme which he must write at once, which he did, in spite of his wife's entreaties. During his illness, he composed five piano variations on this theme. This was his last work.

One of the ideas that occupied his mind was the belief that he 'could never be cured at home', but must resign himself to the cure of some physician. On one occasion he sent for a carriage, arranged his papers and compositions, and prepared to depart. He was perfectly aware of his condition, and, when violently excited, would beg his family to help him. His wife made every effort to dissipate the phantoms and delusions which haunted his fevered imagination. Hardly had she succeeded when some new fancy would disturb his distracted

138

brain. He declared again and again that he was a sinner who did not deserve to be loved. Thus the unhappy master's agony increased, until at last, after a fortnight of terrible struggle against his disease, he gave way, and his sufferings drove him to a desperate step.

On Monday, 27 February 1854, he received a noonday visit from his physician, Dr Hasenclever, and his musical friend, Albert Dietrich. They sat and chatted together sociably. During the conversation, Schumann, without a word, left the room. They supposed he would return; but when some time passed, and he did not come, his wife went in search of him. He was nowhere to be found. His friends hastened out to look for him — in vain. He had left the house in his dressing-gown, with bare head, gone to the bridge that spans the Rhine, and sought to end his misery by plunging into the stream. Some sailors jumped into a boat, rowed after him, and pulled him out. His life was saved, but to what purpose! Passersby recognised the wretched master, and he was carried home. The news was broken to his wife, who was not permitted to see him in his lamentable state. A second physician was called in, for a fearful paroxysm at once ensued, which finally ceased. He now required constant watching.

Wilhelm Joseph von Wasielewski
Life of Robert Schumann

Peter Tchaikovsky

TCHAIKOVSKY TO HIS BROTHER, MODESTE ILYICH

Moscow, 22 September 1876
I have been thinking much, these days, about myself and my future. The result of all these thoughts is that dating from today, I shall make a serious effort to marry, legally, anybody. I am aware that my inclinations are the greatest and most unconquerable obstacle to happiness; I must fight my

nature with all my strength . . . .* I shall do everything
possible to marry this year, and if I am not brave enough for
that, at any rate I shall conquer my old habits for once
and all.

TCHAIKOVSKY TO NADEJDA VON MECK

Moscow, 15 July 1877
For God's sake, dear Nadejda Philaretovna, forgive me for
not writing before. Briefly, here is the story of what has
lately happened to me.

In the latter part of May, to my own great surprise, I
became engaged to be married. This is how it happened.
Some time ago, I received a letter from a girl whom I knew
and had met. From it, I learned that she had honoured me
with her love for a long time. It was written so sincerely and
warmly that I was led to do what in such cases I had always
carefully avoided — to answer. Although my answer did not
give any hope that the feeling could be mutual, the correspondence started. I will not tell you in detail about it, but
the result was that I consented to go to see her. Why did I?
I now feel as if Fate had drawn me to that girl. When I met
her I again explained to her that I felt no more than sympathy and gratitude for her love. And when I left I began to
think over all the giddiness of my behaviour. If I did not care
for her, if I did not want to encourage her, why then did I go
to see her, and how will it all end?

From the next letter I found that if I should suddenly dis-
continue all relations with her after having gone so far, I
would make her most unhappy and drive her to a tragic end.
So I had a difficult alternative — to save my freedom at the
price of the girl's ruin (ruin is not an empty word — she really
loves me to distraction) — or to marry. I could not do otherwise than choose the latter. One thing that helped me to a
decision was the fact that my 82-year-old father and all my
relatives live in the hope of having me marry. So one fine

*The composer is referring to his homosexuality.

140

evening, I went to my future wife, told her frankly that I did not love her, but that I would be a devoted and grateful friend, described my character in detail, my irritability, my variable temperament, unsociability, and finally my circumstances. Then I asked her if she would be my wife. The answer, of course, was 'yes.' I have no words for the feelings I experienced during the days following that evening; it can only be imagined. Having lived thirty-seven years with an antipathy for marriage, it is hard to be goaded by circumstance to the role of a fiancé completely indifferent to his bride. It means altering one's whole life, thinking of the welfare of the person to whom one is united. All this, for an egotistical bachelor, is not easy.

In order to think it over and adjust my mind to such a future, I decided to go to the country for a month, according to my original plan. The quiet country life, surrounded by pleasant people and beautiful nature, had a beneficial influence. I decided that I could not avoid my destiny and that Fate itself had decreed my meeting with this girl. Also, I know from experience that very often in life, what frightens and appals results in good, while on the contrary, the very happiness we have longed for and worked for, disappoints us. Let what is to be, be.

Now let me tell you a little bit about my future wife. Her name is Antonina Ivanovna Miliukoff. She is 28. She is rather attractive. Her reputation is irreproachable. To be independent and free, she supports herself. She has a loving mother. She is quite poor, educated not above the average (she was educated in the Elisabeth Institute) and seems to be very kind, capable of giving herself without reservations.

You ask whether I call you friend. But how can you doubt it? Have you not read again and again between the lines of my letter how deeply I care for your friendship, and that my tenderness for you is very true and warm? How I should like to prove some time, not by word but by deed, all the strength of my gratitude and sincere love for you! Alas I have only one way, my music. Well, in that way, I am always ready to serve you; so why don't you write about the work you wanted me to do? If I cannot always satisfy your wishes as to the composition of one or another piece, because I cannot always be in the mood that is needed for composition, I can always do any other type of musical work. I even urge you, order such things from me as often as possible so that I can, little by little, pay my debt to you.

I shall write on the symphony, 'Dedicated to My Friend', as you have desired.

And so goodbye, my dear, good, sweet friend. Pray that I shall not break under the approaching change in my life. God knows I am filled with the best intentions regarding my future helpmate, and if we are unhappy, it will not be my fault. My conscience is clear. Though I am marrying without love, I do it because circumstances would permit no other course. I giddily accepted the first declaration of love she sent me; I should not have answered her; but once I had encouraged her love by responding and visiting her, I had to do as I did. Anyway, I repeat, my conscience is clear. I have not lied or pretended. I have told her what she can expect from me and on what she must not count. Please do not tell anybody what has led to the marriage. Except you, nobody knows.

Yours,

P.T.

The sound of distant thunder in that final paragraph is unmistakable, even to the most casual reader.

The storm was not long in coming. Less than five months later Tchaikovsky wrote to Nadejda von Meck from Switzerland:

Clarens, 23 October 1877

I spent two weeks with my wife in Moscow. Those two weeks were a series of the most unbearable mental agonies. I saw right away that I could never love my wife, and that the *habit* on which I had counted would never come. I fell into despair

142

and longed for death, which seemed the only way out. I had moments of madness in which my whole being was filled with such terrific distaste for my poor wife that I wanted to strangle her. I could not carry on my work either in the Conservatory or at home. My mind began to go. Yet I knew I alone was to blame. My wife, whatever she may be, is not responsible for my encouraging her and bringing us to the point of marriage. My lack of character, my weakness, blundering and childishness were responsible for everything.

And, shortly after, again to Nadejda Philaretovna:

You must be amazed that I could have bound my life to such a strange companion. I myself cannot explain it. Some madness must have come over me. I imagined that I would surely be affected by her love for me, in which I then believed, and that on my side I could learn to love her. I know now that she never loved me. But one must be just — her wish to marry me, she mistook for love. And then, I repeat, she did everything she could to make me love her. Alas, the more she tried the more she alienated me! I vainly fought this feeling; I knew she did not deserve it, but what could I do with my unruly emotions? Dislike grew not by the day, the hour, but by the minute — little by little becoming a huge, ferocious hate such as I never before felt and of which I did not think myself capable. At last I lost the ability to control myself. What happened next you already know. Just now my wife is with my sister, and soon she will choose a permanent place to live.

Yesterday my brother had a letter from her in which she appears in an absolutely new light. From a gentle dove suddenly she turns into a very ill-natured, demanding person, a liar. She levels many reproaches at me, the gist of which is that I have shamelessly duped her. I have written to her explaining that I do not wish to start any argument, because it will lead us nowhere, and taking all guilt on myself. I begged her to forgive me the wrong I had done her, and said that I yield beforehand to whatever decision she may make, but that live with her I never shall — this I said positively. Certainly it is understood I will see that she is not in need, and I asked her to accept means of support from me. I await an answer. I have spent money enough to take care of her for some time.

This is all I have to tell you about my relations with my wife. Looking back on the short time we lived together, I have come to the conclusion that the *beau role* is entirely hers, not mine. She acted honestly, sincerely, and consistently. She deceived herself by her love, and not me. She was sure, I imagine, that she loved me. As for me, though I had carefully told her that I bore her no love, yet I had promised to do everything I could to love her, and as I arrived at a somewhat contrary result, I was guilty of deluding her. Anyhow, she deserves pity. Judging from yesterday's letter, offended pride has awakened, and has decidedly begun to speak.

Little by little I have started to work, and I can say definitely that our symphony will be finished not later than December, and then you shall hear it. Let this music, so closely connected with your image, tell you that I love you with all my soul, my best friend, my friend-above-all-friends.

Goodbye. Thank you, thank you, dear Nadejda Philaretovna.

Your

P. Tchaikovsky

So far, the correspondence above reveals little more than an embarrassing, and even harrowing, private grief; but the 'symphony' which the composer mentions was completed in spite of all the domestic and sexual agony which beset him.

In a later letter to Nadejda von Meck he attempted to explain in words what the Fourth Symphony in F minor meant to him, and in doing so provided posterity with an extraordinary and unique view both of the work itself and of another aspect of the creative process of composition.

You ask me if this symphony has a definite programme. In reply to this sort of question in reference to a symphony I usually answer no, none. And it is really very difficult to

144

answer such a question. How can one express the indefinable sensations one experiences while writing an instrumental composition that has no definite subject? It is a purely lyrical process. It is a musical confession of the soul, which is full to the brim, and which, true to its nature, unburdens itself through sounds just as a lyric poet expresses himself through poetry. The difference lies in the fact that music has far richer resources of expression and is a more subtle medium into which to translate the thousand shifting moments in the soul's moods. In general, the seed of a future composition appears suddenly and unexpectedly. If the soil is ready — that is to say, if the disposition to work is present — it takes root with astonishing force and swiftness, shoots up through the surface, puts out branches, leaves, and finally blossoms. Only by this metaphor can I describe the creative process. The great problem is that the seed must appear at a favourable moment; the rest takes care of itself. I would try vainly to express in words that unbounded sense of bliss that comes over me when a new idea opens up within me and starts to take on definite form. Then I forget everything and behave like one demented. Everything inside me begins to pulse and quiver: I hardly begin the sketch before one thought begins tumbling over another. In the midst of this magic process it often happens that an interruption from outside awakens me from my somnambulistic condition: someone rings the bell, a servant enters, or a clock strikes, reminding me that it is time to stop. This kind of interruption is truly horrible. Sometimes it breaks off the inspiration for a considerable time, and I have to search for it again, frequently in vain. In such a case cold reason and technical knowledge have to be levied on for assistance. Even with the greatest masters there are often moments when the organic sequence breaks off and a skilful jointure has to be manufactured so that the sections appear to be completely one. But that cannot be avoided. If the state of mind and soul that we call inspiration lasted without interruption for a long time, no artist could survive. The strings would snap and the instrument

145

shatter into fragments. It is already a good thing if the central ideas and the general pattern of a composition come without intense mental activity, appearing as a result of that supernatural and inexplicable force we call inspiration.

However, I have wandered away from the answer to your question. In *our* symphony there is a programme. That is, it is possible for me to outline in words what it attempts to express, and to you, to you alone, I want and am able to communicate the meaning of the whole, as well as of the separate sections. This I can do, of course, in general terms only.

The introduction contains the germ of the entire symphony, without question its central idea:

This is Fate, the fatal force that prevents our striving for happiness from succeeding, that jealously watches to see that felicity and peace shall not be complete or unclouded, that hangs over the head like the sword of Damocles and constantly, unswervingly poisons the soul. It is invincible, it can never be mastered. One must submit to it and take refuge in futile longings.

The unconsolable, hopeless feeling is growing stronger and more consuming. Would it not be better to turn away from reality and immerse oneself in dreams?

Oh joy! A sweet, tender vision has appeared. A blessed, luminous being flies by and beckons somewhere.

146

etc.

How wonderful! How distantly already sounds the importunate first theme of the Allegro. Little by little, dreams have completely enveloped the soul. All that was gloomy and joyless is forgotten. Happiness is here, it is here!

But no! They were only dreams, and Fate awakens us harshly.

etc.

And thus all life is an incessant shifting between grim reality and fleeting visions and reveries of joy. There is no haven. We are buffeted by the waves hither and thither until the sea swallows us. That, approximately, is the programme of the first movement.

The second movement of the symphony expresses another phase of longing. This is the melancholy feeling that suffuses you towards evening when you are sitting alone, weary from work. You have taken a book, but it has fallen from your hands. A host of memories appears. And you are sad because so much is already past. It is pleasant to remember one's youth and to regret the past, but there is no wish to begin again. Life has tired you out. It is pleasant to rest and cast a backward glance. Many things flit through the memory. There were happy moments when young blood pulsed warm and life was gratifying. There were also moments of grief, of irreparable loss. It is all remote in the past. It is both sad and somehow sweet to lose oneself in the past.

The third movement expresses no definite sensations. It is a capricious arabesque, fleeting apparitions that pass through the imagination when one has begun to drink a little wine and is beginning to experience the first phase of intoxication. The soul is neither happy nor said. You are not thinking of anything; the imagination is completely free and for some reason has begun to paint curious pictures. . . . Among them you suddenly remember some muzhiks on a spree, and a street song. Then somewhere in the distance a military parade is moving along. These are the disconnected images that pass through our heads as we begin to fall asleep. They have nothing in common with reality, they are strange, exotic, incoherent.

The fourth movement. If you cannot discover reasons for happiness in yourself, look at others. Get out among the people. Look, what a good time they have, surrendering themselves to joy! A picture of popular merriment on a holiday. You have scarcely had a chance to forget yourself when indefatigable Fate appears once more and reminds you of herself. But the others pay no attention to you. They do not even turn around, do not even look at you, do not notice that you are alone and sad. Oh, how gay they are! How fortunate they are that their emotions are direct and uncomplicated! Upbraid yourself and do not say that all the world is sad. Strong, simple joys exist. Take happiness from the joys of others. Life is bearable after all.

I can tell you nothing more, dear friend, about the symphony. My description is naturally neither clear nor satisfactory. But that is the peculiarity of instrumental music — it cannot be analysed. As Heine said, 'Where words leave off, music begins.'

Letters taken from
Tchaikovsky by **Herbert Weinstock**

Chopin

Chopin's turbulent relationship with the unconventional authoress George Sand, the love of his mature life, inspired and infuriated him by turn. The final rift between them came as a result of a family quarrel in which Chopin took the part
148

of Sand's daughter Solange, which George regarded as disloyal.

Here are two accounts of their last meeting, both, broadly speaking, factually correct, but which, placed side by side, provide a fascinating insight into the almost infinite options open to a biographer.

Chopin and Sand saw each other only once again. Their accounts of the meeting tally. Chopin had been visiting Charlotte Marliani; as he was leaving he ran into George accompanied by Lambert in the vestibule. Chopin bowed and asked, 'Have you had news from Solange lately?'

'A week ago,' Sand replied.

'No news yesterday or the day before?'

'No.'

'Then permit me to tell you that you have become a grand-mother. Solange has a baby girl and I am very glad to be the first to give you the news.'

Chopin then tipped his hat, and accompanied by an acquaintance nicknamed the Abyssinian, he walked downstairs. Then he remembered that he had said nothing to Sand about her daughter's condition. So he asked the Abyssinian to go upstairs again, saying that he was too feeble to reclimb the stairs — perhaps this was a pretext to avoid seeing Sand a second time — and to tell George that Solange and the baby were well. Later he wrote to Solange:

5 March [1848]

I was waiting below for the Abyssinian when your mother came down with him and showed great interest in asking me about your health. I replied that you *yourself* had written me a pencilled note the day after your child was born. I said you had suffered a great deal but the sight of your baby girl had made you forget it all. She asked whether your husband was with you, and I replied that the address on your letter seemed to be in his handwriting. She asked how I was — I said I was

149

well, and then I called for the concierge to open the door. I raised my hat and walked back home to the Square d'Orléans, accompanied by the Abyssinian.

George R. Marek and Maria Gordon-Smith
Chopin

Louis-Philippe fled from Paris, the monarchy fell and the second Republic was proclaimed. The excitement in Paris, the shooting, barricades and general uproar left Chopin almost unmoved. He disliked the idea of a Republic and at first was afraid of disorders in the streets and annoyances from 'the People', But quietness and order were soon restored. A much more interesting event was the birth of Solange's daughter. She sent him a pencil note to say that though she had suffered a great deal all was well now, and Chopin's thoughts were very much taken up with considering whether this would not improve the relations between George and her daughter.

The day after he received this news he went with a friend of the name of Combes to call on Mme Marliani in order to discuss with her the possibilities of the situation. He found her, however, surrounded by other visitors — it was impossible to have any confidential conversation — and the only thing of interest that he heard was that Mme Sand had hurried up to Paris to take part in the revolution, and was staying in a hotel near Maurice.

The thought that she was in Paris agitated him. He wanted to go home to adjust his ideas and emotions, and after a very short visit he signed to Combes to come away and they took their departure. As they opened the door of the flat to go out, Chopin found himself face to face with George Sand, coming with Lambert to call on Mme Marliani.

His mind was so full of her that it was hardly a surprise; but the suddenness of her appearance made his heart beat quickly — while his breath came and went in jerks. He thought

150

violently that he must keep calm, that he must not let her see what he was feeling, and in the voice — as he told himself — in which one greets a stranger, he said: 'Bonjour, madame.'

She answered as calmly and distantly, and in the seconds this had taken he had resolved on what he was to do.

'Forgive me for asking, but is it long since you have had news of Mme Clésinger?' he asked.

She looked somewhat surprised, but answered immediately.

'That last time I heard was a week ago.'

'You heard nothing yesterday? The day before yesterday . . .?'

'No.'

'Then I must inform you that you are a grandmother. Solange has a little girl, and I am very glad to be the first to tell you the news.'

Hastily bowing he hurried down the stairs followed by the startled Combes. But having reached the ground floor he realised that he had said nothing about the health of either mother or child . . . how stupid . . . she would be anxious . . . she must be told. Climbing the stairs again was, however, out of the question; he turned to Combes.

'Dear Combes,' he panted, 'would you be kind enough to go back and tell Mme Sand that Mme Clésinger and the baby are both well? It was idiotic of me to forget to say so. . . .'

'Certainly,' replied Combes, and disappeared.

Chopin leant against the wall in a tumult of thought. She looked exactly as she had done the last time he saw her . . . she had not smiled . . . she had been calm — grave — beautiful. He shut his eyes, but hearing steps opened them again and saw Combes, and beside him, George.

'Solange is well?' she asked, with a touch of eagerness. 'Have you heard any details?'

'I have had a pencil note from her, in her own handwriting, written the day after the birth of the child. She said she had suffered a great deal, but the sight of the little girl made her forget it all.'

A smile broke slowly over George's face and then faded again.

151

'Was her husband with her at the time?'

'I imagine so, for the letter looked as if it was addressed in his handwriting.'

There was a pause, and George took a step towards him.

'How are you, Frédéric?' she said in a low voice. 'You have been ill . . . are you better now?'

Her physical nearness increased his agitation so much that he was conscious only of the necessity of leaving her.

'I am very well,' he replied hurriedly; and turning to the hall porter, 'please open the door.'

George came nearer still and without speaking held out her hand. He took it. His own was icy cold and trembling, and he could not look at her. The door was open, and bowing hastily he passed out without another word. Combes took his arm and led him back to the Square d'Orléans. He hardly noticed it, he hardly noticed that Combes had left him, his mind was full of George — her face, her voice, her smile, the touch of her hand; he repeated over and over again in his thoughts that brief interview, and presently the passionate desire came over him to recount it all to someone else — in that way he would almost relive the scene, almost experience again her presence, her contact. But it was impossible, the episode had been too pointless to tell a third person — and then suddenly he thought of Solange — to her the tale would be full of interest and meaning.

He quickly sat down and wrote a letter to her. It was hardly more than a minute account of every detail that had occurred. The elaborate chronicle was just what he wanted to give outlet to his feelings. He folded and sealed the letter, and then rose with a sigh of relief and sat down at the piano . . . he played a few notes . . . suddenly put down his head on the desk of the piano and began to sob.

Marjorie Strachey
The Nightingale

152

The truth is that every great composer, without exception, has been appreciated, admired, applauded, and loved in his own time. Even those who died miserably, died famous.

Henry Pleasants
The Agony of Modern Music, 1955

The strain involved by his arduous labours at Prague was increased by the indifference with which his opera, *La Clemenza di Tito,* was received, and Mozart returned to Vienna with spirits depressed, and mind and body exhausted by overwork. Nevertheless, he braced himself anew, and on 30 September the new opera, *Die Zauberflöte* ('The Magic Flute'), was produced. Though somewhat coldly received at first, the work increased in popularity at each subsequent representation, until its success was everything that could be desired. A friend who had a place in the orchestra on the first performance relates that he was so enchanted with the overture that he crept up to the chair in which Mozart sat conducting, and, seizing the composer's hand, pressed it to his lips. Mozart glanced kindly at him, and, extending his right hand, gently stroked his cheek.

The *Requiem* was still far from finished, and to this work Mozart now turned his attention. But it was too late; the strain and excitement which he had undergone during the past few months had done their work, a succession of fainting fits followed, and it was evident that the marvellous powers

153

which he had controlled in the past were no longer under his command. With fast-fleeting strength came the oppressive thought, haunting him from day to day, that he would not live to complete the work. 'It is for myself that I am writing this *Requiem*,' he said one day to Constanze, whilst his eyes filled with tears. Vainly she endeavoured to comfort him; he declared that he felt his end approaching, and, indeed, death — the 'best and truest friend' — was very near him now, far nearer than they who gathered about his bed, and sought to cheer him with the news that his freedom from anxiety was at last to be assured by the combined action of the nobility in securing to him an annuity — far nearer than they, or other well-wishers, whose tardy recognition of his claims had come too late, imagined. He who had 'always hovered between hope and anxiety' was now hovering between life and death, soon to be released from all earthly travail.

On the evening of 4 December they brought the score of the *Requiem* to him at his request, and, propped up by pillows, he began to sing one of the passages, in company with three of his friends. They had not proceeded far, however, before Mozart laid the manuscript aside, and, bursting into tears, declared that it would never be finished. A few hours later, at one o'clock in the morning of 5 December 1791, he passed away in sleep.

The body was removed from the house on the following day, and taken to St Stephen's Church, where it received benediction. The hearse, with the few mourners, then proceeded to St Mark's churchyard, but before the burial place was reached a terrific storm of snow and rain burst overhead, and with one accord the followers turned back, and left the hearse to proceed alone. And thus the master of whom it was prophesied that he would cause all others to be forgotten — he whose triumphs had caused him to be acclaimed by thousands as '*grande* Mozart' — was left to be buried by the hands of strangers in a pauper's grave, without even a stone to mark the spot where he was laid.

And to this day no one knows exactly which is the resting-place of Wolfgang Amadeus Mozart.

Francis Jameson Rowbotham
Story Lives of Great Musicians

I have occasionally remarked that the only entirely creditable incident in English history is the sending of £100 to Beethoven on his deathbed by the London Philharmonic Society; and it is the only one that historians never mention.

George Bernard Shaw
Letter to *The Times,* 20 December 1932

Standing by the grave of him who has passed away we are in a manner the representatives of an entire nation, of the whole German people, mourning the loss of the one highly acclaimed half of that which was left us of the departed splendour of our native art, of the fatherland's full spiritual bloom. There yet lives — and may his life be long — the hero of verse in German speech and tongue; but the last master of tuneful song, the organ of soulful concord, the heir and amplifier of Handel and Bach's, of Haydn and Mozart's immortal fame is now no more, and we stand weeping over the riven strings of the harp that is hushed.

He was an artist, but a man as well. A man in every sense — in the highest. Because he withdrew from the world, they called him a man-hater, and because he held aloof from sentimentality, unfeeling. Ah, one who knows himself hard of heart, does not shrink! The finest points are those most easily blunted and bent or broken. An excess of sensitiveness avoids a show of feeling! He fled the world because, in the whole range of his loving nature, he found no weapon to oppose it. He withdrew from mankind after he had given them his all

155

and received nothing in return. He dwelt alone, because he found no second Self. But to the end his heart beat warm for all men, in fatherly affection for his kindred, for the world his all and his heart's blood.

Thus he was, thus he died, thus he will live to the end of time.

You, however, who have followed after us hitherward, let not your hearts be troubled! You have not lost him, you have won him. No living man enters the halls of the immortals. Not until the body has perished, do their portals unclose. He whom you mourn stands from now onward among the great of all ages, inviolate forever. Return homeward therefore, in sorrow, yet resigned! And should you ever in times to come feel the overpowering might of his creations like an onrushing storm, when your mounting ecstasy overflows in the midst of a generation yet unborn, then remember this hour, and think, We were there, when they buried him, and when he died, we wept.

Franz Grillparzer
Funeral Oration quoted in *Thayer's Life of Beethoven*

The American poet and composer Stephen Collins Foster died destitute in New York in 1864, aged 37. Among over 175 songs he wrote are 'My Old Kentucky Home', 'Oh Susanna', 'Old Folks at Home', 'Beautiful Dreamer', 'Camptown Races' and 'Old Black Joe'.

The Bellevue Hospital listed the personal possessions of the dead composer as follows: 'Coat, pants, vest, hat, shoes, over-coat.' The total assets of his purse were thirty-eight cents, and a slip of paper on which he had pencilled the words: 'Dear friends and gentle hearts'.

'Personal Recollections of the Last Days of Foster', by **Mrs Parkhurst Duer**:

I shall never forget the day I met him. I was engaged in a

large music publishing house on Broadway, New York City, leading a very busy life, although but 21 years of age. Every day I met teachers and composers, and was ever hoping Stephen Foster would appear. I had heard that he was living in New York but had never known anything about his life; yet his songs had created in me a feeling of reverence for the man, and I longed to see him. One day I was speaking with the clerks, when the door opened, and a poorly dressed, very dejected man came in and leaned against the counter near the door, I noticed he looked ill and weak. No one spoke to him. A clerk laughed and said:

'Steve looks down and out.'

Then they all laughed, and the poor man saw them laughing at him. I said to myself, Who can Steve be? It seemed to me, my heart stood still. I asked, 'Who is that man?'

'Stephen Foster,' the clerk replied. 'He is only a vagabond, don't go near him.'

'Yes, I will go near him, that man needs a friend,' was my reply.

I was terribly shocked. Forcing back the tears, I waited for that lump in the throat which prevents speech to clear away. I walked over to him, put out my hand, and asked, 'Is this Mr Foster?'

He took my hand and replied: 'Yes, the wreck of Stephen Collins Foster.'

'Oh, no,' I answered, 'not a wreck, but whatever you call yourself, I feel it an honour to take by the hand, the author of 'Old Folks at Home', I am glad to know you.'

As I spoke, the tears came to his eyes, and he said: 'Pardon my tears, young lady, you have spoken the first kind words I have heard in a long time. God bless you.'

I gave him both hands, saying: 'They will not be the last.' I asked him to sit at my desk awhile, and get acquainted. (He seemed pleased, but apologised for his appearance. He was assured it was not his dress, but Mr Foster I wanted to see.) I judged him to be about 45 years of age, but the lines of care upon his face and the stamp of disease gave him that appearance. We had a long conversation. (I told him of the effect his music had upon me, since my childhood, and how I had longed to know him.) He opened his heart to me, and gave me an insight of his true character, which greatly increased my admiration, but which cannot be repeated in a writing of this length. Stephen Foster was a man of culture and refinement. . . .

When this first visit was ended, Mr Foster thanked me for my interest in him, and said it had done him a world of good to have someone to talk with. He had no one to call a friend. I asked him to let me be a friend, and perhaps in my humble way, I might be of service to him. I said if he would bring me the manuscript songs that he had not been able to write out, I would do the work for him at his dictation. He was very grateful, and from that time until he died I was permitted to be his helper. Out of respect for my efforts to aid Mr Foster, all the men in the store treated him kindly. He was made welcome, and no one laughed at him. They were convinced he was no vagabond, and no drunkard. He was poor; disease brought poverty; he had been unable to write, and soon his personal appearance caused him to be misjudged. No hand was stretched out to rescue him in a great Christian community. I dared not question him concerning his comforts in life, or how he existed, but I was confident he needed help, yet how to aid without humiliating him was a study.

When he brought me his rude sketches, written on wrapping paper picked up in a grocery store, and he told me he wrote them while sitting upon a box or barrel, I knew he had no home. I asked him if he had a room; he said:

'No — I do not write much, as I have no material or conveniences.' He then told me that he slept in the cellar room of a little house, owned by an old couple, down in Elizabeth Street in the 'Five Points', who knew who he was. and charged him nothing. He said he was comfortable, so I suppose he had a bed. Then I told him that unless he had the right kind of food, he could not be restored to health, and a kind manager of a nearby restaurant had arranged to provide him with a

158

hearty dinner every day, and he need not pay for anything until he was able to do business, and a friend had sent him some medicine which he must take. He looked at me for a moment and that fervent 'God bless you', paid for all the planning. It was an easy matter to provide other necessary comforts, to be paid for when he recovered his health. We who were near him had no hope of his recovery, but the few comforts provided lessened the suffering of a dying man. This messenger of song God had given to the world was not appreciated, and when overtaken by misfortune, was treated as other great souls in the past, left to die, forsaken by a nation he had blessed by his living.

The Étude
September 1916

Foster, by the end of his life a hopeless alcoholic, died estranged from his family and his wife. Her name was Jane. . . .

I long for Jeanie with the day-dawn smile,
Radiant in gladness, warm with winning guile;
I hear her melodies, like joys gone by,
Sighing 'round my heart o'er the fond hopes that die:
Sighing like the night wind and sobbing like the rain,
Waiting for the lost one that comes not again:
Oh! I dream of Jeanie with the light brown hair,
Floating, like a vapour, on the soft summer air.

Stephen Foster
'Jeanie with the light brown hair'

With wonderful deathless ditties
We build up the world's great cities,
　　And out of a fabulous story
　　We fashion an empire's glory:
One man with a dream, at pleasure,
　　Shall go forth and conquer a crown;
And three with a new song's measure
　　Can trample an empire down.

Arthur William Edgar O'Shaughnessy

Acknowledgements

The author and publishers are most grateful to the following for granting us permission to reproduce extracts in this book: Victor Gollancz Ltd (A.L. Bacharach, *The Musical Companion*); Penguin Books Ltd (Hector Berlioz, *Evenings in the Orchestra*); Margaret Ramsay Ltd (Robert Bolt, record sleeve material on Lady Caroline Lamb); Oxford University Press (Deryck Cooke, *The Language of Music*); A.P. Watt Ltd (Robin Daniels, *Conversations with Cardus*); Faber & Faber Ltd (Eric Fenby, *Delius as I Knew Him*); Princeton University Press (Elliot Forbes, *rev. & ed. Thayer's Life of Beethoven*); Hamish Hamilton Ltd and W.W. Norton Inc. (Derek Jewell, *Duke*); *Gramophone* (Walter Legge, 'Dinu Lipatti'); London Magazine Editions (Bryan Magee, *Aspects of Wagner*); Macdonald and Co Ltd and Alfred Knopf Inc. (Yehudi Menuhin, *Unfinished Journey*); Victor Gollancz Ltd (James Methuen-Campbell, *Chopin Playing*); John Myers (letter to Robin Ray); David & Charles Ltd (Gerald Norris, *A Musical Gazetteer of Great Britain and Ireland*); David Higham Associates (Robert Payne, *Gershwin*); *The Daily Telegraph* (Peterborough extract, 8.5.84); CBS Masterworks (Charles Rosen, record sleeve material on Ravel's 'Gaspard de la Nuit'/'Tombeau de Couperin'); Jonathan Cape Ltd and Alfred Knopf Inc. (Artur Rubinstein, *My Young Years*); John Farquharson Ltd (Harold Schonberg, *The Great Pianists* and *The Great Conductors*); Hutchinson Books Ltd (Boris Schwartz, *Music and Musical Life in Soviet Russia*); Doubleday Inc. (Nat Shapiro, *Encyclopaedia of Quotations about Music*); University of Washington Press (Slonimsky, *Lexicon of Musical Invective*); Elaine Greene Ltd and Harper & Row Inc. (Marek and Gordon Smith, *Chopin*); Penguin Books Ltd (Hamish Swanston, *In Defence of Opera*); Oxford University Press (Sir Donald Tovey, *Essays in Musical Analysis*); A. & C. Black Ltd (W.J. Turner, *Music — A Short History*); Michael Joseph Ltd and Simon & Schuster Inc. (W.J. Turner, *The Groucho Letters*); Macmillan London Ltd

(Hugh Vickers, *Great Operatic Disasters*); Harry Winstanley (Godowsky Society Newsletter); Victor Gollancz Ltd (Henry Wood, *My Life of Music*); EMI Records (Public letter concerning Dinu Lipatti and Halina Czerny-Stefanska): Guinness Books ('The Most Prolific Composer of All Time'); EMI Records (record sleeve material, 'Cortot Plays Chopin'); The Society of Authors ('Radio Music' from George Bernard Shaw's Music); *The Guardian; Radio Times.*

The publishers have made every effort to trace copyright holders in the following works, but as it has not been possible to do so in every case we apologise for any errors or omissions: Claudio Arrau and Joseph Horowitz, *Conversations with Arrau* (Wm. Collins Sons and Co Ltd); Leonard Bernstein, *The World in Vogue*; Donald Brook, *Conductors Gallery, Masters of the Keyboard* and *Violinists of Today* (Rockliff); Cyril Clarke (ed.), *The Composer in Love* (Peter Neville Ltd); Mike Edwards, 'My Favourite Composer is Opus' (*Music Journal*); Peter Gammond, *Bluff Your Way in Music*; Eduard Hanslick, *Music Criticisms* (Peregrine Books); Anthony Hopkins, *Music All Around Me*; John Tasker Howard, *Stephen Foster* (Thomas and Cornwell, NY); Harry James, TV 'Obituary' programme, 5.7.83; Anselm Huttenbrenner, *Franz Schubert, the Man and his Circle*; Hubert Kupferberg, *The Fabulous Philadelphians*; Oscar Levant, *The Memoirs of an Amnesiac*; John Julius Norwich, *A Christmas Cracker* (private publication); Mrs Parkhurst Duer, *Personal Recollections of the Last Days of Foster*, Henry Pleasants, *The Agony of Modern Music*; André Previn, *Music Face to Face*, (ed.) *Orchestra* (Macdonald and Jane's); Sergei Rachmaninoff, *My Prelude in C Sharp Minor*; Robin Ray, 'Don't Smile at the Brass' (*View* magazine); Francis Jameson Rowbotham, *Story Lives of Great Musicians* (Wells Gardner and Co Ltd); Royal Festival Hall, programme note on Arturo Benedetti Michelangeli; Roy Robertson, *Musical Suggestions for 'The King of Kings'*; Tony Thomas, *Music for the Movies* (Tantivy Press, NY); Leon Vallas, *Claude Debussy — his life and works*; Wilhelm Joseph von Wasielaski, *Life of Robert Schumann*; Otto Zoff, *Great Composers through the Eyes of their Contemporaries* (E.P. Dutton Inc., N.Y.); quotes from Pierre Boulez, Arnold Schoenberg and Jascha Heifetz.

Index

169